Third Edition

ITALIAN VERB DRILLS

Paola Nanni-Tate

New York Chicago San Francisco Lisbon London Madrid Mexico City
Milan New Delhi San Juan Seoul Singapore Sydney Toronto

1 2 3 4 5 6 7 8 9 10 11 12 13 14 15   WDQ/WDQ   1 9 8 7 6 5 4 3 2 1 0

ISBN 978-0-07-174473-7
MHID   0-07-174473-8

Library of Congress Control Number: 2010925176

McGraw-Hill books are available at special quantity discounts to use as premiums and sales promotions or for use in corporate training programs. To contact a representative, please e-mail us at bulksales@mcgraw-hill.com.

Bonus Online Exercises

Supplemental exercises, featuring more than 100 questions, can be found at mhprofessional.com.

Simply follow these easy steps:

1. Go to mhprofessional.com.
2. Search for "Italian Verb Drills, Third Edition," or "9780071744737" (the book's ISBN).
3. Click on the "Launch" icon underneath the book's cover image.

This book is printed on acid-free paper.

Table of Contents

Introduction

Italian Verb Drills has been written for students of the Italian language who wish to take the time to master the structures and the conjugations of Italian verbs by learning the rules and doing the numerous exercises outlined in this book.

Italian Verb Drills covers verb tenses from the present indicative to the past subjunctive, and each tense is preceded by rules and examples to clarify its use. An answer key is supplied for the students to check their knowledge and progress, and the Indexes of Verbs list all the verbs covered in the book.

While *Italian Verb Drills* is not intended to cover "all" Italian verbs, it lists a large number of the verbs that are commonly used.

Italian Verb Drills will also serve as an example and a guide to learn other verbs that follow similar patterns.

This book has been inspired and encouraged by my husband, Bob, and by all my students, especially the ones who have studied Italian with me for a long time. To all of them I give my thanks and I dedicate *Italian Verb Drills*.

Paola Nanni-Tate

Chapter 1

Overview of Italian Verbs

1. Verb Structure

All Italian verbs have four moods: (1) The *infinitive* expresses the action itself, with no reference to time or person. It is the form given in the dictionary. (2) The *indicative* expresses a thing as a fact, and it is the most commonly used mood. It has several tenses. (3) The *imperative* is used to give orders. It has one tense (present), and it is in the 2nd person (you) with singular and plural forms, and familiar and polite forms. The 1st person plural such as *andiamo* (let's go), *mangiamo* (let's eat) is also considered imperative. (4) The *subjunctive* expresses *possibility, hopes, feelings, wishes,* and it is almost always preceded by *che,* such as in *che io venga* (that I come).

Italian verbs have two numbers: singular and plural. They have three persons.

	Singular			**Plural**		
1st person	*io*	*mangio*	I eat	*noi*	*mangiamo*	we eat
2nd person	*tu*	*mangi*	you eat	*voi*	*mangiate*	you eat
3rd person	*lui, lei*	*mangia*	he, she eats	*loro*	*mangiano*	they eat

2. Subject Pronouns (Pronomi Personali)

In English, the subject pronouns are always used: *I, you, he, she, it, we, you, they.* In Italian, as a general rule, they are seldom needed since the endings of the verbs give the information about the person doing the action. Only in the 3rd person singular and the 3rd person plural could there be some confusion, so it is advisable to use *lui* (he), *lei* (she), *loro* (they). *It* can be translated with *esso* or *essa,* but nowadays these forms are not very commonly used.

In Italian, there are several ways to say **you**: In the singular, there are the informal *tu* and the formal *Lei,* which is used for both men and women and which is followed by the 3rd person singular of the verb. In the plural, *Loro* and the 3rd person plural of the verb are used when talking to more than one person formally and informally. *Voi* may also be used.

Examples:	Do you speak English?
Singular:	
Informal	(Tu) parli inglese?
Formal	(Lei) parla inglese?
Plural:	
Informal	(Voi) parlate inglese?
Formal	(Loro) parlano inglese?

3. Interrogative in Italian

Usually, there is no change in the word order in Italian when asking a question, only a change of intonation when speaking, and a question mark when writing. The **do, does, did** in English are not translated.

Example: Do you (informal) remember?   (Tu) ricordi?

4. Negative in Italian

The negative in Italian is formed by putting **non** in front of the verb. In compound tenses, **non** is placed in front of the auxiliary verb.

Examples: *Non mangio niente.*   I don't eat anything.
    Non abbiamo parlato con lui.   We didn't speak with him.

5. Infinitive and the Three Conjugations

All Italian verbs end in *-are, -ere,* or *-ire* in their infinitives.

Verbs ending in *-are* (*mangiare,* to eat) are in the *1st conjugation.*
Verbs ending in *-ere* (*vedere,* to see) are in the *2nd conjugation.*
Verbs ending in *-ire* (*sentire,* to hear) are in the *3rd conjugation.*

Verbs Ending in *-are*

6. Present Tense of *-are* Verbs

The *present indicative* of regular verbs in the 1st conjugation (*-are* verbs) is formed by adding *o, i, a, iamo, ate, ano* to the root of the verb. The root is obtained by dropping the *-are* ending from the infinitive.

Parlare		**Mangiare**	
Singular:			
io parl*o*	I speak	io mangi*o*	I eat
tu parl*i*	you speak	tu mang*i*	you eat
lui parl*a*	he speaks	lui mangi*a*	he eats
lei parl*a*	she speaks	lei mangi*a*	she eats
Plural:			
noi parl*iamo*	we speak	noi mangi*amo*	we eat
voi parl*ate*	you speak	voi mangi*ate*	you eat
loro parl*ano*	they speak	loro mangi*ano*	they eat

Note: *Lei parla, lei mangia* are used for **she speaks, she eats,** or the formal, 2nd person singular, *you speak, you eat.*

Most verbs in the 1st conjugation are regular. (Some very common irregular ones are studied later in this chapter.) A few have some spelling differences.

a. Verbs ending in *-care, -gare,* like *cercare* (to look for) and *pagare* (to pay), add *h* before endings with *i* or *e* to maintain the same sound of the root of the verb.

   Examples: *cerco* (I look for), *cerchi* (you look for).

b. Verbs ending in *-ciare, -giare,* like *cominciare* (to begin) and *mangiare* (to eat), omit *i* before endings with *e* or *i.*

   Examples: *mangio* (I eat), *mangi* (you eat), not *mangii.*

c. Verbs ending in *-iare* omit the *i* ending of the 2nd person singular of the present tense if the *i* is not in the accented syllable.

   Examples: For *studiare* (to study), forms are *studio, studi,* and not *studii.* For *avviare* (start) forms are *avvio, avvii,* and not *avvi!*

7. List of Common *-are* Verbs

Here are some common regular verbs ending in *-are.*

abitare	to live	**litigare**	to quarrel
aiutare	to help	**mandare**	to send
arrivare	to arrive	**mostrare**	to show
ascoltare	to listen	**notare**	to notice
aspettare	to wait	**nuotare**	to swim
ballare	to dance	**pagare**	to pay
cambiare	to change	**pensare**	to think
camminare	to walk	**portare**	to bring
cantare	to sing	**pranzare**	to have lunch
cenare	to have supper	**provare**	to try
cominciare	to start	**raccontare**	to narrate
contare	to count	**rallentare**	to slow down
dimenticare	to forget	**regalare**	to give a gift
domandare	to ask	**ricordare**	to remember
fermare	to stop, to close	**riposare**	to rest
giocare	to play	**ritornare**	to return
girare	to turn	**saltare**	to jump
guidare	to drive	**spiegare**	to explain
gustare	to taste	**studiare**	to study
imparare	to learn	**suonare**	to play
insegnare	to teach	**tagliare**	to cut
lasciare	to leave, to let	**trovare**	to find
lavare	to wash	**viaggiare**	to travel
lavorare	to work	**volare**	to fly

8. Practice

Note: All regular verbs ending in **-are** form the present indicative like the models in part 6. Write the **present tense** of the verbs.

1. **cantare**   io _____   tu _____   lui, lei _____

    (to sing)   noi _____   voi _____   loro _____

2. **provare**   io _____   tu _____   lui, lei _____

    (to try)   noi _____   voi _____   loro _____

3. **lavorare**   io _____   tu _____   lui, lei _____

    (to work)   noi _____   voi _____   loro _____

4. **ricordare**   io _____   tu _____   lui, lei _____

    (to remember)   noi _____   voi _____   loro _____

5. **viaggiare**   io _____   tu _____   lui, lei _____

    (to travel)   noi _____   voi _____   loro _____

6. **volare**   io _____   tu _____   lui, lei _____

    (to fly)   noi _____   voi _____   loro _____

9. Practice

Write the *present tense* of the verbs in the person indicated by the pronoun.

Io:

studiare	insegnare	viaggiare	saltare
_____	_____	_____	_____

Tu:

parlare	mangiare	trovare	ballare
_____	_____	_____	_____

Lui, Lei:

imparare	entrare	lavare	riposare
_____	_____	_____	_____

Noi:

comprare	arrivare	aiutare	tagliare
_____	_____	_____	_____

Voi:

parlare	imparare	aspettare	pensare
_____	_____	_____	_____

Loro:

spiegare	insegnare	contare	camminare
_____	_____	_____	_____

10. Practice

Write the *present tense* of the verb in the person indicated by the pronoun.

1. Noi (mangiare) _____

2. Lui (imparare) _____

3. Loro (comprare) _____

4. Io (cantare) _____

5. Tu (camminare) _____

6. Voi (parlare) _____

7. Noi (studiare) _____

8. Lei (cambiare) _____

9. Voi (pensare) _____

10. Lei (nuotare) _____

11. Io (giocare) _____

12. Noi (pranzare) _____

13. Voi (viaggiare) _____

14. Loro (ballare) _____

15. Lei (lavorare) _____

16. Noi (lavare) _____

17. Io (pensare) _____

18. Noi (imparare) _____

19. Io (ascoltare) _____

20. Lei (amare) _____

21. Voi (abitare) _____

22. Loro (pagare) _____

23. Tu (entrare) _____

24. Noi (ispezionare) _____

25. Lui (pensare) _____

26. Tu (mandare) _____

11. Practice

Rewrite in English in the right form and person.

1. Mangiamo _____

2. Imparo _____

3. Comprano _____

4. Canto _____

5. Cammini _____

6. Parlate _____

7. Studiamo _____

8. Cambio _____

9. Pensate _____

10. Nuoto _____

11. Gioco _____

12. Pranziamo _____

13. Viaggiate _____

14. Ballano _____

15. Lavora _____

16. Laviamo _____

17. Penso _____

18. Impariamo _____

19. Ascolto _____

20. Ama _____

21. Abitate _____

22. Pagano _____

23. Entri _____

24. Ispezioniamo _____

25. Pensa _____

26. Mandi _____

12. Practice

Rewrite in Italian.

1. I eat _____

2. You (s.) think _____

3. They learn _____

4. We sing _____

5. You (pl.) eat _____

6. He studies _____

7. She teaches _____

8. I learn _____

9. You (s.) work _____

10. They wash _____

11. She enters _____

12. We rest _____

13. You (s.) wait _____

14. They sing _____

15. I dance _____

16. We jump _____

17. I travel _____

18. He finds _____

19. We arrive _____

20. You (pl.) wait _____

21. She helps _____

22. I buy _____

23. She finds _____

24. We study _____

Negative and Interrogative Forms

Rewrite in Italian.

1. I don't eat _____

2. You (s.) don't work _____

3. We don't remember _____

4. They don't work _____

5. She doesn't enter _____

6. I don't rest _____

7. Do you (s.) eat? _____

8. Do you (s.) work? _____

9. Do we remember? _____

10. Do they work? _____

11. Does she enter? _____

12. Do I rest? _____

13. Practice

Rewrite in English.

1. Parliamo _____

2. Salti _____

3. Pensa _____

4. Cantate _____

5. Suono _____

6. Mangiamo _____

7. Imparano _____

8. Trovi _____

9. Entriamo _____

10. Lavori _____

11. Insegniamo _____

12. Lavate _____

13. Riposo _____

14. Guarda _____

15. Camminiamo _____

16. Portate _____

17. Balli _____

18. Parlano _____

19. Viaggia _____

20. Aiutiamo _____

21. Ricordo _____

22. Dimentica _____

23. Non mangio _____

24. Non camminano _____

25. Non lavorate _____

26. Lavori? _____

14. Irregular Verbs Ending in -are

In the 1st conjugation, there are four irregular verbs:

stare	to stay	**fare**	to make, to do
dare	to give	**andare**	to go

The following are the conjugation of these irregular verbs:

Stare

io	sto	I stay
tu	stai	you stay
lui	sta	he stays
lei	sta	she stays
noi	stiamo	we stay
voi	state	you stay
loro	stanno	they stay

Dare

io	do	I give
tu	dai	you give
lui	dà	he gives
lei	dà	she gives
noi	diamo	we give
voi	date	you give
loro	danno	they give

Fare

io	faccio	I make, I do
tu	fai	you make, you do
lui	fa	he makes, he does
lei	fa	she makes, she does
noi	facciamo	we make, we do
voi	fate	you make, you do
loro	fanno	they make, they do

Andare

io	vado	I go
tu	vai	you go
lui	va	he goes
lei	va	she goes
noi	andiamo	we go
voi	andate	you go
loro	vanno	they go

15. Practice

Write the *present tense* of the verbs.

1. **dare**   io _____   tu _____   lui, lei _____

   (to give)   noi _____   voi _____   loro _____

2. **fare**   io _____   tu _____   lui, lei _____

   (to make, do)   noi _____   voi _____   loro _____

3. **stare**   io _____   tu _____   lui, lei _____

   (to stay)   noi _____   voi _____   loro _____

4. **andare**   io _____   tu _____   lui, lei _____

   (to go)   noi _____   voi _____   loro _____

Chapter 2

Verbs Ending in *-ere*

1. Present Tense of *-ere* Verbs

All the verbs ending in *-ere,* such as **temere** (to fear), belong to the 2nd conjugation. The **present** indicative of verbs in the 2nd conjugation is formed by adding *o, i, e, iamo, ete, ono* to the root of the verb.

Vedere	To see		**Scrivere**	To write
io ved*o*	I see		io scriv*o*	I write
tu ved*i*	you see		tu scriv*i*	you write
lui ved*e*	he sees		lui scriv*e*	he writes
lei ved*e*	she sees		lei scriv*e*	she writes
noi ved*iamo*	we see		noi scriv*iamo*	we write
voi ved*ete*	you see		voi scriv*ete*	you write
loro ved*ono*	they see		loro scriv*ono*	they write

In the present tense of some *-ere* verbs, the pronunciation changes, but the spelling of the root and the endings stay the same. In verbs ending in **-cere** and **-gere,** such as **vincere** (to win) and **leggere** (to read), the pronunciation changes to a hard sound when the *o* or *a* follows *c* or *g.*

Examples: Vinc*o,* vinci, vince, vinciamo, vincete, vinc*ono*
                  Legg*o,* leggi, legge, leggiamo, leggete, legg*ono*

2. List of Common *-ere* Verbs

Here are some common verbs ending in *-ere.*

accadere	to happen	**esistere**	to exist
accedere	to access	**godere**	to enjoy
accendere	to turn on	**includere**	to include
apprendere	to learn	**insistere**	to insist
assistere	to assist	**leggere**	to read
assolvere	to absolve	**mettere**	to put
assumere	to assume, hire	**nascondere**	to hide
attendere	to wait for, attend	**perdere**	to lose
cadere	to fall	**permettere**	to allow
cedere	to yield	**piangere**	to cry
chiedere	to ask	**prendere**	to take
chiudere	to close	**pretendere**	to pretend
comprendere	to comprehend	**promettere**	to promise
concludere	to conclude	**promuovere**	to promote
condividere	to share	**ridere**	to laugh
confondere	to confuse	**risolvere**	to resolve
conoscere	to know	**rispondere**	to answer
consistere	to consist	**rompere**	to break
convincere	to convince	**scendere**	to descend
correggere	to correct	**scrivere**	to write
correre	to run	**sorridere**	to smile
credere	to believe	**spingere**	to push
crescere	to grow	**succedere**	to happen
decidere	to decide	**temere**	to fear
difendere	to defend	**trasmettere**	to broadcast
discutere	to discuss	**vedere**	to see
distinguere	to distinguish	**vincere**	to win
dividere	to divide	**vivere**	to live

Note: Some of the above verbs are irregular in other forms, but they all form the *present indicative* with the regular endings.

3. Practice

Note: Most verbs in *-ere* form the present tense like the above models in part 1.
Write the *present tense* of the verbs.

1. **dividere**   io _____   tu _____   lui, lei _____

   (to divide)   noi _____   voi _____   loro_____

2. **chiudere**   io _____   tu _____   lui, lei _____

   (to close)   noi _____   voi _____   loro_____

3. **mettere**   io _____   tu _____   lui, lei _____

   (to put)   noi _____   voi _____   loro_____

4. **convincere**   io _____   tu _____   lui, lei _____

   (to convince)   noi _____   voi _____   loro_____

5. **spingere**   io _____   tu _____   lui, lei _____

   (to push)   noi _____   voi _____   loro_____

6. **perdere**   io _____   tu _____   lui, lei _____

   (to lose)   noi _____   voi _____   loro_____

4. Practice

Write the present tense of the verbs in the person indicated.

Io:

apprendere   attendere   chiedere   chiudere

_____   _____   _____   _____

Tu:

cadere   confondere   dividere   crescere

_____   _____   _____   _____

Lui, Lei:

decidere   difendere   discutere   concludere

_____   _____   _____   _____

Noi:

apprendere   attendere   insistere   esistere

_____   _____   _____   _____

Voi:

cadere   ridere   rispondere   nascondere

_____   _____   _____   _____

Loro:

perdere   piangere   insistere   promettere

_____   _____   _____   _____

5. Practice

Rewrite in Italian.

1. I fear _____

2. You (s.) wait for _____

3. He falls _____

4. We ask _____

5. You (s.) assist _____

6. He closes _____

7. They confuse _____

8. You (s.) know _____

9. They decide _____

10. He defends _____

11. She discusses _____

12. We decide_____

13. He asks _____

14. You (s.) enjoy _____

15. I conclude _____

16. She insists_____

17. We put _____

18. He loses _____

19. I promise _____

20. We promise _____

21. We cry _____

22. They answer _____

23. I see _____

24. She sees _____

25. I write _____

26. I cry _____

Negative and Interrogative Forms

Rewrite in Italian.

1. I don't assist_____

2. You don't (s.) wait for _____

3. We don't ask _____

4. They don't divide_____

5. She doesn't close _____

6. He doesn't cry _____

7. Do you (s.) assist? _____

8. Do you (s.) wait for?_____

9. Do you (s.) ask?_____

10. Do they divide? _____

11. Do you (s.) close? _____

12. Do you (s.) cry?_____

6. Practice

Rewrite in English.

1. Apprendiamo _____
2. Teme _____
3. Assumiamo _____
4. Attendono _____
5. Cado _____
6. Credete _____
7. Chiede _____
8. Chiudono _____
9. Correggi _____
10. Concludete _____
11. Condividono _____
12. Confondono _____
13. Conosci _____
14. Conoscono _____
15. Cuocete _____
16. Cuoce _____
17. Decido _____
18. Difendete _____
19. Discutiamo _____
20. Includiamo _____
21. Insiste _____
22. Perdete _____
23. Perdono _____
24. Piangono _____
25. Pretende _____
26. Rispondi _____
27. Vedo _____
28. Vinci _____
29. Conosce _____
30. Vincono _____
31. Ridete _____
32. Rompono _____
33. Non rimango _____
34. Non permettono _____
35. Non leggiamo _____
36. Leggete? _____
37. Leggi? _____
38. Vediamo? _____
39. Scrive? _____
40. Temono? _____
41. Non vedete? _____
42. Non leggi? _____
43. Non scrivono? _____
44. Non scriviamo? _____

7. Irregular Verbs Ending in -ere

In the 2nd conjugation, there are many irregular verbs. Here are some of the most common.

Bere	To drink	**Cogliere**	To gather
io bevo	I drink	*io* colgo	I gather
tu bevi	you drink	*tu* cogli	you gather
lui beve	he drinks	*lui* coglie	he gathers
lei beve	she drinks	*lei* coglie	she gathers
noi beviamo	we drink	*noi* cogliamo	we gather
voi bevete	you drink	*voi* cogliete	you gather
loro bevono	they drink	*loro* colgono	they gather

Dovere	Must, to have to	**Porre**	To put
io devo	I must/have to	*io* pongo	I put
tu devi	you must/have to	*tu* poni	you put
lui deve	he must/has to	*lui* pone	he puts
lei deve	she must/has to	*lei* pone	she puts
noi dobbiamo	we must/have to	*noi* poniamo	we put
voi dovete	you must/have to	*voi* ponete	you put
loro devono	they must/have to	*loro* pongono	they put

Potere	To be able	**Rimanere**	To stay
io posso	I am able	*io* rimango	I stay
tu puoi	you are able	*tu* rimani	you stay
lui può	he is able	*lui* rimane	he stays
lei può	she is able	*lei* rimane	she stays
noi possiamo	we are able	*noi* rimaniamo	we stay
voi potete	you are able	*voi* rimanete	you stay
loro possono	they are able	*loro* rimangono	they stay

Sapere	To know	**Scegliere**	To choose
io so	I know	*io* scelgo	I choose
tu sai	you know	*tu* scegli	you choose
lui sa	he knows	*lui* sceglie	he chooses
lei sa	she knows	*lei* sceglie	she chooses
noi sappiamo	we know	*noi* scegliamo	we choose
voi sapete	you know	*voi* scegliete	you choose
loro sanno	they know	*loro* scelgono	they choose

Sedere	To sit	**Spegnere**	To turn off
io siedo	I sit	*io* spengo	I turn off
tu siedi	you sit	*tu* spegni	you turn off
lui siede	he sits	*lui* spegne	he turns off
lei siede	she sits	*lei* spegne	she turns off
noi sediamo	we sit	*noi* spegniamo	we turn off
voi sedete	you sit	*voi* spegnete	you turn off
loro siedono	they sit	*loro* spengono	they turn off

Tenere	To keep	Volere	To want
io tengo	I keep	*io voglio*	I want
tu tieni	you keep	*tu vuoi*	you want
lui tiene	he keeps	*lui vuole*	he wants
lei tiene	she keeps	*lei vuole*	she wants
noi teniamo	we keep	*noi vogliamo*	we want
voi tenete	you keep	*voi volete*	you want
loro tengono	they keep	*loro vogliono*	they want

8. Practice

Write the *present tense* of the verbs.

1. **dovere**   io _____   tu _____   lui, lei _____
   (must)   noi _____   voi _____   loro _____

2. **scegliere**   io _____   tu _____   lui, lei _____
   (to choose)   noi _____   voi _____   loro _____

3. **potere**   io _____   tu _____   lui, lei _____
   (to be able)   noi _____   voi _____   loro _____

4. **sapere**   io _____   tu _____   lui, lei _____
   (to know)   noi _____   voi _____   loro _____

5. **tenere**   io _____   tu _____   lui, lei _____
   (to keep)   noi _____   voi _____   loro _____

6. **volere**   io _____   tu _____   lui, lei _____
   (to want)   noi _____   voi _____   loro _____

Verbs Ending in *-ire*

9. Present Indicative of *-ire* Verbs

All the verbs ending in **ire,** such as **partire** (to depart, to leave) and **dormire** (to sleep), belong to the 3rd conjugation.

The *present indicative* of verbs in the 3rd conjugation is formed by adding *o, i, e, iamo, ite, ono* to the root of the verb. Many verbs of the 3rd conjugation insert *isc* between the root and the endings of the present tense.

Dormire		To sleep	**Finire**		To finish
io	dorm*o*	I sleep	io	fin*isco*	I finish
tu	dorm*i*	you sleep	tu	fin*isci*	you finish
lui	dorm*e*	he sleeps	lui	fin*isce*	he finishes
lei	dorm*e*	she sleeps	lei	fin*isce*	she finishes
noi	dorm*iamo*	we sleep	noi	fin*iamo*	we finish
voi	dorm*ite*	you sleep	voi	fin*ite*	you finish
loro	dorm*ono*	they sleep	loro	fin*iscono*	they finish

The following *-ire* verbs do not insert *isc* when conjugated:

acconsentire	to agree	**fuggire**	to escape
applaudire	to applaud	**inghiottire**	to swallow
aprire	to open	**inseguire**	to follow
assentire	to agree, to consent	**investire**	to invest
avvertire	to announce	**mentire**	to lie
bollire	to boil	**offrire**	to offer
conseguire	to result	**partire**	to leave, depart
consentire	to agree	**seguire**	to follow
convertire	to convert	**sentire**	to hear
coprire	to cover	**servire**	to serve
divertire	to enjoy	**soffrire**	to suffer
eseguire	to do	**vestire**	to dress

The following *-ire* verbs insert *isc* in the present tense of the indicative.

aderire	to adhere	**guarire**	to heal
attribuire	to attribute	**impazzire**	to go mad
benedire	to bless	**inserire**	to insert
capire	to understand	**istruire**	to instruct
colpire	to hit	**preferire**	to prefer
costruire	to build	**pulire**	to clean
definire	to define	**punire**	to punish
digerire	to digest	**restituire**	to return
dimagrire	to lose weight	**riunire**	to meet
esaurire	to exhaust	**sostituire**	to substitute
esibire	to exhibit	**spedire**	to send
fallire	to fail	**stabilire**	to establish
ferire	to wound	**suggerire**	to suggest
finire	to finish	**tradire**	to betray
garantire	to guarantee	**trasferire**	to transfer
gestire	to manage	**ubbidire**	to obey

Note: Some of the above verbs are irregular, but they all form the present indicative with regular endings.

10. Practice

Most verbs ending in *-ire* form the present indicative like the models on page 21.
Write the *present tense* of the verbs.

1. **avvertire**   io _____   tu _____   lui, lei _____

   (to notify)   noi _____   voi _____   loro _____

2. **bollire**   io _____   tu _____   lui, lei _____

   (to boil)   noi _____   voi _____   loro _____

3. **sentire**   io _____   tu _____   lui, lei _____

   (to hear)   noi _____   voi _____   loro _____

4. **capire**   io _____   tu _____   lui, lei _____

   (to understand)   noi _____   voi _____   loro _____

5. **preferire**   io _____   tu _____   lui, lei _____

   (to prefer)   noi _____   voi _____   loro _____

11. Practice

Write the *present tense* of the following *-ire* verbs in the indicated person.

Io:

aprire	capire	offrire	finire
_____	_____	_____	_____

Tu:

dormire	avvertire	bollire	sentire
_____	_____	_____	_____

Lui, Lei:

preferire	partire	vestire	spedire
_____	_____	_____	_____

Noi:

servire	vestire	aprire	capire
_____	_____	_____	_____

Voi:

avvertire	seguire	costruire	istruire
_____	_____	_____	_____

Loro:

sentire	inseguire	investire	partire
_____	_____	_____	_____

12. Practice

Rewrite in Italian.

1. I prefer_____
2. You (s.) consent_____
3. He covers _____
4. We enjoy_____
5. They escape_____
6. He understands_____
7. He follows_____
8. You (s.) lie _____
9. I hear_____
10. We suffer_____
11. They open_____
12. He finishes _____

13. You (s.) applaud_____
14. He converts_____
15. I applaud_____
16. He sleeps_____
17. I swallow _____
18. You (pl.) leave _____
19. They serve _____
20. I sleep _____
21. She prefers _____
22. I understand _____
23. We prefer _____
24. I build _____

Negative and Interrogative Forms

Rewrite in Italian.

1. I don't finish_____
2. He doesn't understand _____
3. They don't instruct_____
4. You (s.) don't hear_____
5. I don't sleep _____
6. We don't applaud_____
7. We don't leave _____
8. I don't suffer_____

9. Do we build? _____
10. Does he hear?_____
11. Do they understand? _____
12. Do they hear?_____
13. Does he sleep? _____
14. Do you consent?_____
15. Does she finish?_____
16. Do we depart? _____

13. Practice

Rewrite in English.

1. Acconsenti _____
2. Applaudono _____
3. Apre _____
4. Aprono _____
5. Avvertiamo _____
6. Bolle _____
7. Capisco _____
8. Consentite _____
9. Convertono _____
10. Copro _____
11. Costruisce _____
12. Offre _____
13. Divertiamo _____
14. Dormite _____
15. Seguono _____
16. Finiamo _____
17. Fugge _____
18. Guarisci _____
19. Garantiscono _____
20. Inghiotti _____
21. Inseguono _____
22. Istruisce _____
23. Preferiscono _____
24. Seguite _____
25. Pulite _____
26. Puniscono _____
27. Colpisce _____
28. Servo _____
29. Soffre _____
30. Sostituisco _____
31. Spediamo _____
32. Sostituiscono _____
33. Suggeriamo _____
34. Trasferiscono _____

Negative and Interrogative Forms

1. Non dormiamo _____
2. Non soffre _____
3. Non capiamo _____
4. Non istruisce _____
5. Non apri _____
6. Acconsenti? _____
7. Partono? _____
8. Dormi? _____
9. Capisci? _____
10. Pulite? _____

14. Irregular Verb Endings in *-ire*

In the 3rd conjugation, there are many irregular verbs. The most common are:

dire	to tell, say	*udire*	to hear
morire	to die	*uscire*	to go out, exit
salire	to go up, ascend	*venire*	to come

The following are the conjugations of the present indicative of the above verbs:

Dire — To tell, say

io	dico	I tell, say
tu	dici	you tell, say
lui	dice	he tells, says
lei	dice	she tells, says
noi	diciamo	we tell, say
voi	dite	you tell, say
loro	dicono	they tell, say

Morire — To die

io	muoio	I die
tu	muori	you die
lui	muore	he dies
lei	muore	she dies
noi	moriamo	we die
voi	morite	you die
loro	muoiono	they die

Salire — To climb

io	salgo	I climb
tu	sali	you climb
lui	sale	he climbs
lei	sale	she climbs
noi	saliamo	we climb
voi	salite	you climb
loro	salgono	they climb

Udire — To hear

io	odo	I hear
tu	odi	you hear
lui	ode	he hears
lei	ode	she hears
noi	udiamo	we hear
voi	udite	you hear
loro	odono	they hear

Uscire — To go out

io	esco	I go out
tu	esci	you go out
lui	esce	he goes out
lei	esce	she goes out
noi	usciamo	we go out
voi	uscite	you go out
loro	escono	they go out

Venire — To come

io	vengo	I come
tu	vieni	you come
lui	viene	he comes
lei	viene	she comes
noi	veniamo	we come
voi	venite	you come
loro	vengono	they come

15. Practice

Write the *present tense* of the verbs.

1. **venire**   io _____   tu _____   lui, lei _____

   (to come)   noi _____   voi _____   loro _____

2. **dire**   io _____   tu _____   lui, lei _____

   (to say)   noi _____   voi _____   loro _____

3. **uscire**   io _____   tu _____   lui, lei _____

   (to go out)   noi _____   voi _____   loro _____

16. Practice

Rewrite in Italian.

1. you (s.) say _____   9. they climb _____

2. they go out _____   10. we go out _____

3. we come _____   11. you (pl.) climb _____

4. they die _____   12. he dies _____

5. I climb _____   13. you (s.) hear _____

6. she says _____   14. they say _____

7. I go out _____   15. we hear _____

8. they come _____   16. you (pl.) say _____

Chapter 3

Imperative

1. Uses of the Imperative: Familiar Forms

The *imperative* is for commands and orders. It is used in the *tu* and *voi* forms, *tu* for singular, familiar and *voi* for the plural, familiar. The forms are similar to the present tense except for the *tu* form of the 1st conjugation, which ends in *a* instead of *i*.

> **Examples:** *parla* (speak) instead of *parli, mangia* (eat), instead of *mangi*

The 1st person plural of the present tense can be used in the imperative, but it is mostly a suggestion and an urgent request rather than a command.

> **Examples:** *scriviamo* (let's write), *mangiamo* (let's eat), *andiamo* (let's go)

The negative *imperative* for *tu* is formed by *non* + the infinitive of the verb.

> **Example:** *Non parlare* (don't speak), *non andare* (don't go)

For the 2nd person plural or *voi, non* is put in front of the *imperative* form.

> **Example:** *Non parlate* (don't speak), *non scrivete* (don't write)

> **Note:** The formal forms of the imperative are introduced on page 32.

2. Familiar Imperative Forms

parla (speak)	*scrivi* (write)	*pulisci* (clean)
parliamo (let's speak)	*scriviamo* (let's write)	*puliamo* (let's clean)
parlate (speak pl.)	*scrivete* (write pl.)	*pulite* (clean pl.)

Negative:

non parlare (don't speak)	*non scrivere* (don't write)	*non pulire* (don't clean)
non parlate (don't speak pl.)	*non scrivete* (don't write pl.)	*non pulite* (don't clean pl.)

3. Practice

Rewrite in Italian in the imperative. Use the singular form unless plural (pl.) is indicated.

1. Speak _____

2. Sing _____

3. Go (pl.) _____

4. Don't go _____

5. Let's go _____

6. Don't eat (pl.) _____

7. Let's finish _____

8. Don't play (pl.) _____

9. Play _____

10. Look _____

11. Listen _____

12. Don't leave _____

13. Let's leave _____

14. Play (pl.) _____

15. Let's play _____

16. Go out _____

17. Don't go out (pl.) _____

18. Play _____

19. Don't play _____

20. Eat (pl.) _____

21. Write _____

22. Don't write _____

23. Let's write _____

24. Close _____

25. Don't close _____

26. Let's close _____

27. Sleep _____

28. Sleep (pl.) _____

29. Drink _____

30. Drink (pl.) _____

31. Read _____

32. Let's read _____

33. Don't read _____

34. Don't read (pl.) _____

4. Practice

Rewrite in English.

1. Parlate _____
2. Canta _____
3. Non cantare _____
4. Ascolta _____
5. Ascoltate _____
6. Andiamo _____
7. Parla _____
8. Non parlare _____
9. Giochiamo _____
10. Non giocate _____
11. Uscite _____
12. Non uscire _____
13. Mangia _____
14. Mangiamo _____
15. Chiudi _____
16. Chiedete _____
17. Pensa _____
18. Non pensate _____
19. Suggerisci _____
20. Parti _____
21. Mettete _____
22. Non mettere _____
23. Spera _____
24. Entrate _____
25. Studia _____
26. Non studiare _____
27. Non partite _____
28. Canta _____
29. Cantiamo _____
30. Spingi _____
31. Non spingere _____
32. Prendete _____

5. Irregular Imperative

There are a few irregular verbs with an irregular *tu* form of the imperative. They are:

	Imperative	
andare (to go)	*và* or *vai*	
avere (to have)	*abbi*	*abbiate* (irregular plural)
dare (to give)	*dà* or *dai*	
dire (to say, to tell)	*dì*	
essere (to be)	*sii*	*siate* (irregular plural)
stare (to stay)	*stà* or *stai*	

6. The *Lei* and *Loro* Forms of the Imperative

The *imperative* for *Lei* and *Loro* is the same as the 3rd person of the present subjunctive (chapter 7). These forms are the formal polite forms.

	Parlare	*Scrivere*	*Sentire*	*Finire*
Lei	*parli*	*scriva*	*senta*	*finisca*
Loro	*parlino*	*scrivano*	*sentano*	*finiscano*

Examples:

Singular:

Parli con la signora!	Speak with the lady!
Scriva subito la lettera!	Write the letter immediately!
Senta la radio!	Listen to the radio!
Finisca di mangiare!	Finish eating!

Plural:

Parlino con la signora!	Speak with the lady!
Scrivano subito!	Write immediately!
Sentano la radio!	Listen to the radio!
Finiscano di mangiare!	Finish eating!

Many of the common verbs have irregular command forms for the polite singular and plural. Following are the most common.

	Singular	**Plural**
andare (to go)	*vada*	*vadano*
bere (to drink)	*beva*	*bevano*
dare (to give)	*dia*	*diano*
dire (to tell, say)	*dica*	*dicano*
fare (to do, to make)	*faccia*	*facciano*
stare (to stay)	*stia*	*stiano*
temere (to fear)	*tema*	*temano*
venire (to come)	*venga*	*vengano*

The *negative imperative* formal is formed by placing *non* before the affirmative.

Examples:	*Non parli!*	Don't speak!
	Non scrivano!	Don't write!

Object and reflexive pronouns *always precede* the *Lei* and *Loro* forms.

Examples:	*Mi scriva!*	Write me!
	Non mi scriva!	Don't write to me!

7. Practice

Rewrite in English, using the *polite forms* of the *imperative* singular and plural as indicated.

1. Wait (s.) _____
2. Wait (pl.)_____
3. Pay (s.) _____
4. Pay (pl.)_____
5. Eat (s.) _____
6. Answer (pl.) _____
7. Finish (s.) _____
8. Look (pl.) _____
9. Come (s.) _____
10. Eat (pl.)_____
11. Answer (s.) _____
12. Finish (pl.)_____
13. Come (pl.)_____
14. Go out (s.) _____
15. Leave (pl.)_____
16. Tell me (s.)_____
17. Think (s.) _____
18. Go out (pl.)_____
19. Walk (s.)_____
20. Sing (pl.)_____
21. Read (pl.) _____
22. Smile (s.) _____

Future

8. Forms of the Future

The *future tense* in Italian consists of a single verb while in English it consists of the auxiliary *shall* or *will* and the infinitive of the verb. The future of regular verbs is formed by putting the future endings on the infinitive of the verb without the final *e*. In the 1st conjugation, the *a* of the infinitive ending changes to *e* in the future.

Examples: *Parlare* (to speak)   *Scrivere* (to write)   *Sentire* (to hear)
              Parlerò (I'll speak)   *Scriverò* (I'll write)   *Sentirò* (I'll hear)

Parlare	**Scrivere**	**Sentire**
io parler*ò*	io scriver*ò*	io sentir*ò*
tu parler*ai*	tu scriver*ai*	tu sentir*ai*
lui parler*à*	lui scriver*à*	lui sentir*à*
lei parler*à*	lei scriver*à*	lei sentir*à*
noi parler*emo*	noi scriver*emo*	noi sentir*emo*
voi parler*ete*	voi scriver*ete*	voi sentir*ete*
loro parler*anno*	loro scriver*anno*	loro sentir*anno*

Note: The 1st and the 3rd persons singular have an accent on the ending. This means that the last syllable must be stressed.

Verbs ending in **-care** and **-gare** add an *h* to the future tense stem to keep the hard *c* and *g* sounds.

Examples: *Pagare* (to pay)   *Io pagherò* (I'll pay)
              Giocare (to play)   *Io giocherò* (I'll play)

Verbs ending in **-ciare** and **-giare** drop the *i* in the future tense stem.

Examples: *Cominciare* (to begin)   *Io comincerò* (I'll begin)
              Mangiare (to eat)   *Io mangerò* (I'll eat)

Here are some verbs that have irregular stems in the future. The endings are the same as the regular future endings.

Infinitive	**Future Stem**	**Conjugation**
andare (to go)	*andr*	andrò, andrai, andrà, etc.
avere (to have)	*avr*	avrò, avrai, avrà, etc.
bere (to drink)	*berr*	berrò, berrai, berrà, etc.
cadere (to fall)	*cadr*	cadrò, cadrai, cadrà, etc.
dare (to give)	*dar*	darò, darai, darà, etc.
essere (to be)	*sar*	sarò, sarai, sarà, etc.
fare (to make)	*far*	farò, farai, farà, etc.
porre (to put)	*porr*	porrò, porrai, porrà, etc.
sapere (to know)	*sapr*	saprò, saprai, saprà, etc.
tenere (to hold)	*terr*	terrò, terrai, terrà, etc.
vedere (to see)	*vedr*	vedrò, vedrai, vedrà, etc.
venire (to come)	*verr*	verrò, verrai, verrà, etc.

9. Practice

Write the *future* tense of the verbs.

1. **vedere**   io _____   tu _____   lui, lei _____
    (to see)   noi _____ voi _____ loro _____

2. **andare**   io _____   tu _____   lui, lei _____
    (to go)   noi _____ voi _____ loro _____

3. **capire**   io _____   tu _____   lui, lei _____
    (to understand)   noi _____ voi _____ loro _____

4. **aiutare**   io _____   tu _____   lui, lei _____
    (to help)   noi _____ voi _____ loro _____

10. Practice

Write the verbs in the *future* tense in the person indicated.

Io:

parlare   vedere   pulire

_____   _____   _____

Tu:

viaggiare   permettere   capire

_____   _____   _____

Lui, Lei:

trovare   sapere   sentire

_____   _____   _____

Noi:

guardare   bere   finire

_____   _____   _____

Voi:

lavorare   avere   partire

_____   _____   _____

Loro:

andare   essere   sentire

_____   _____   _____

11. Practice

Rewrite in English.

1. Capirò _____
2. Lavorerò _____
3. Leggerai _____
4. Canterà _____
5. Sentirete _____
6. Pianterai _____
7. Ascolterò _____
8. Pianterete _____
9. Vedremo _____
10. Risponderanno _____
11. Pagherò _____
12. Giocheremo _____
13. Penserai _____
14. Vedrete _____
15. Sentirai _____
16. Deciderò _____
17. Piangeremo _____
18. Vincerà _____
19. Discuterete _____

20. Andremo _____
21. Studierò _____
22. Penserete _____
23. Scriverai _____
24. Cuocerò _____
25. Finirò _____
26. Giocheremo _____
27. Staremo _____
28. Farai _____
29. Darete _____
30. Partirai _____
31. Direte _____
32. Dormiremo _____
33. Inseguirai _____
34. Verremo _____
35. Bollirò _____
36. Applaudiranno _____
37. Aprirà _____
38. Saliremo _____

Negative Future Forms

Rewrite in English.

1. Non mangerò _____
2. Non andremo _____
3. Non farà _____

4. Non canteremo _____
5. Non capirà _____
6. Non finirete _____

12. Practice

Rewrite in Italian.

1. I'll attend _____
2. He'll fall _____
3. We'll write _____
4. They'll think_____
5. We'll understand _____
6. I'll close _____
7. You'll (s.) speak_____
8. We'll play_____
9. They'll travel _____
10. I'll put_____
11. We'll do _____
12. He'll find _____
13. We'll find _____
14. I'll listen _____
15. We'll learn _____
16. I'll eat _____
17. We'll go _____
18. They'll make _____
19. I'll stay _____
20. I'll buy _____

21. They'll come _____
22. I'll come _____
23. We'll look_____
24. We'll say_____
25. He'll tell _____
26. They'll sing _____
27. We'll cry_____
28. I'll plant _____
29. We'll go out_____
30. They'll climb _____
31. You'll (pl.) go _____
32. We'll follow _____
33. He'll insist _____
34. She'll see _____
35. We'll answer_____
36. I'll pay _____
37. We'll vote_____
38. I'll decide _____
39. We'll drink_____
40. We'll hear_____

Negative Future Forms

Rewrite in Italian.

1. I won't eat _____
2. He won't listen _____

3. We won't drink _____
4. They won't eat_____

Chapter 4

Imperfect

1. Uses of the Imperfect

This is a very easy tense to learn, but not so easy to use.

In Italian, the *imperfect* is always used to refer to an action in the past that is continuing while another takes place.

Example:	Mentre *parlavo,* tu arrivasti.	While I *was speaking,* you came.

The *imperfect tense* in Italian expresses the English *used to.*

Example:	*Parlavo.*	I used to speak.

With verbs of *thinking, believing,* and *feeling,* the imperfect is generally used rather than the other past forms—the *past definite (passato remoto)* or the *present perfect (passato prossimo),* found in future lessons.

Examples:	*Volevo* scrivere.	I wanted to write.
	Mi *sentivo* male.	I felt bad.

The *imperfect* is used to describe actions or conditions that lasted for an indefinite period of time in the past. In English, this is the same as the form expressed by *was* and the *ing* form of the verb.

Examples:	*Leggevo* il giornale.	I *was reading* the newspaper.
	Guardavo la televisione.	I *was watching* television.

The *imperfect* is used to express habitual action in the past, and it is usually preceded or followed by words such as *di solito, qualche volta, spesso, sempre.*

Examples:	*Studiava sempre* con la sua amica.	She used to always study with her friend.
	Di solito, *guardavo* la televisione.	Usually, I would watch TV.

The *imperfect* tense is used to describe time, age, weather, in the past.

Example:	*Faceva* bel tempo/brutto tempo.	The weather was nice/bad.

2. Forms of the Imperfect

The *imperfect* is formed by adding the same endings to all three conjugations. The only difference among the conjugations is the typical vowel of the infinitive.

parlare—parl*avo*   (To speak—I used to speak)
credere—cred*evo*   (To believe—I used to believe)
finire—fin*ivo*   (To finish—I used to finish)

Parlare To speak	**Vedere** To see	**Dormire** To sleep
io parl*avo*	io ved*evo*	io dorm*ivo*
tu parl*avi*	tu ved*evi*	tu dorm*ivi*
lui parl*ava*	lui ved*eva*	lui dorm*iva*
lei parl*ava*	lei ved*eva*	lei dorm*iva*
noi parl*avamo*	noi ved*evamo*	noi dorm*ivamo*
voi parl*avate*	voi ved*evate*	voi dorm*ivate*
loro parl*avano*	loro ved*evano*	loro dorm*ivano*

3. Practice

Write the *imperfect tense* of the verbs.

1. **pensare**   io _____   tu _____   lui, lei _____
    (to think)   noi _____   voi _____   loro _____

2. **bere**   io _____   tu _____   lui, lei _____
    (to drink)   noi _____   voi _____   loro _____

3. **finire**   io _____   tu _____   lui, lei _____
    (to finish)   noi _____   voi _____   loro _____

4. **abitare**   io _____   tu _____   lui, lei _____
    (to live)   noi _____   voi _____   loro _____

4. Practice

Write the verbs in the *imperfect tense* in the person indicated.

Io:

mangiare   mettere   sentire

_____   _____   _____

Tu:

cantare   vedere   finire

_____   _____   _____

Lui, Lei:

saltare   bere   aprire

_____   _____   _____

Noi:

votare   rispondere   costruire

_____   _____   _____

Voi:

giocare   comprendere   applaudire

_____   _____   _____

Loro:

sperare   vendere   preferire

_____   _____   _____

5. Practice

A. Write the *imperfect* of the verbs.

1. Lui (parlare) _____

2. Voi (cantare) _____

3. Lui (abitare) _____

4. Noi (partire) _____

5. Voi (giocare) _____

6. Loro (finire) _____

7. Io (camminare) _____

8. Tu (perdere) _____

9. Voi (comprendere) _____

10. Loro (mangiare) _____

11. Tu (costruire) _____

12. Voi (istruire) _____

13. Lui (lavorare) _____

14. Lei (ballare) _____

15. Loro (pensare) _____

16. Voi (credere) _____

17. Tu (lavare) _____

18. Noi (scrivere) _____

19. Io (correre) _____

20. Lei (parlare) _____

B. Rewrite in English.

1. Mangiavamo _____

2. Studiavi _____

3. Bevevi _____

4. Giocavi _____

5. Sentiva _____

6. Capivate _____

7. Scrivevano _____

8. Chiedevo _____

9. Chiudevate _____

10. Ascoltava _____

11. Prendevamo _____

12. Imparavo _____

13. Vendevamo _____

14. Vendevi _____

15. Capivi _____

16. Vivevano _____

17. Istruiva _____

18. Vedeva _____

19. Ricevevano _____

20. Insegnavo _____

6. Practice

Rewrite in Italian, using the *imperfect*.

1. They used to eat _____
2. We were thinking_____
3. You (s.) were coming _____
4. I believed _____
5. They didn't think _____
6. I was learning _____
7. They believed_____
8. We used to ask _____
9. You (s.) didn't want _____
10. He was waiting _____
11. They were learning _____
12. I understood _____
13. You could _____
14. We used to sing_____
15. They wanted_____
16. I thought _____
17. We thought_____
18. He wanted_____
19. He used to go_____
20. I was waiting _____
21. I was hoping _____
22. We used to hope _____
23. I used to speak_____

24. Were you studying?_____
25. Were you speaking?_____
26. He was hoping _____
27. You (s.) thought_____
28. We were working _____
29. They wanted_____
30. We used to look_____
31. Were we looking? _____
32. He used to travel _____
33. I was teaching _____
34. They used to eat _____
35. I didn't understand_____
36. I couldn't _____
37. They used to sing _____
38. They didn't want _____
39. I didn't think _____
40. You (s.) thought_____
41. She wanted _____
42. I used to clean _____
43. We were looking _____
44. They weren't hoping _____
45. He was hoping _____
46. You (s.) doubted _____

Passato Remoto (Preterit)

7. Uses of the Passato Remoto

The *passato remoto* is a past tense, also called the historical past. It is mostly used in narrative writing of events of the past.

The *passato remoto* and the *passato prossimo* (a compound tense found in the next chapter) are similar since they both express an action in the past. They are commonly translated into English by the simple past, e.g., I bought, we played.

The *passato prossimo* is commonly used in speaking about the past. On the other hand, the *passato remoto* is mostly used in writing but is sometimes used in speaking, when the action is considered distant and not connected to the present.

8. Forms of the Passato Remoto

The *passato remoto* is formed by putting the correct endings to the infinitive roots. Following are the endings of the *passato remoto* for the three conjugations. Many common verbs have irregular roots for the *passato remoto*.

Comprare To buy	**Vendere** To sell	**Sentire** To hear
io compr*ai*	vend*ei*	sent*ii*
tu compr*asti*	vend*esti*	sent*isti*
lui compr*ò*	vend*è*	sent*ì*
lei compr*ò*	vend*è*	sent*ì*
noi compr*ammo*	vend*emmo*	sent*immo*
voi compr*aste*	vend*este*	sent*iste*
loro compr*arono*	vend*erono*	sent*irono*

9. Practice

Write the *passato remoto* of the verbs.

1. **mangiare**   io _____   tu _____   lui, lei _____
   (to eat)   noi _____   voi _____   loro _____

2. **potere**   io _____   tu _____   lui, lei _____
   (to be able)   noi _____   voi _____   loro _____

3. **capire**   io _____   tu _____   lui, lei _____
   (to understand)   noi _____   voi _____   loro _____

10. Common Verbs with Irregular Roots in the Passato Remoto

Many common verbs have irregular roots in the *passato remoto* and they must be learned. The endings are the same as previously shown. Following are some of the most common verbs with irregular roots for the *passato remoto.*

Accendere:	*Accesi, accendesti, accese, accendemmo, accendeste, accesero*
Bere:	*Bevvi, bevesti, bevve, bevemmo, beveste, bevvero*
Cadere:	*Caddi, cadesti, cadde, cademmo, cadeste, caddero*
Chiedere:	*Chiesi, chiedesti, chiese, chiedemmo, chiedeste, chiesero*
Chiudere:	*Chiusi, chiudesti, chiuse, chiudemmo, chiudeste, chiusero*
Cogliere:	*Colsi, cogliesti, colse, cogliemmo, coglieste, colsero*
Conoscere:	*Conobbi, conoscesti, conobbe, conoscemmo, conosceste, conobbero*
Dare:	*Diedi, desti, diede, demmo, deste, diedero*
Decidere:	*Decisi, decidesti, decise, decidemmo, decideste, decisero*
Dire:	*Dissi, dicesti, disse, dicemmo, diceste, dissero*
Discutere:	*Discussi, discutesti, discusse, discutemmo, discuteste, discussero*
Dovere:	*Dovetti, dovesti, dovette, dovemmo, doveste, dovettero*
Fare:	*Feci, facesti, fece, facemmo, faceste, fecero*
Leggere:	*Lessi, leggesti, lesse, leggemmo, leggeste, lessero*
Mettere:	*Misi, mettesti, mise, mettemmo, metteste, misero*
Nascere:	*Nacqui, nascesti, nacque, nascemmo, nasceste, nacquero*
Prendere:	*Presi, prendesti, prese, prendemmo, prendeste, presero*
Porre:	*Posi, ponesti, pose, ponemmo, poneste, posero*
Ridere:	*Risi, ridesti, rise, ridemmo, rideste, risero*
Rimanere:	*Rimasi, rimanesti, rimase, rimanemmo, rimaneste, rimasero*
Sapere:	*Seppi, sapesti, seppe, sapemmo, sapeste, seppero*
Scegliere:	*Scelsi, scegliesti, scelse, scegliemmo, sceglieste, scelsero*
Scendere:	*Scesi, scendesti, scese, scendemmo, scendeste, scesero*
Scrivere:	*Scrissi, scrivesti, scrisse, scrivemmo, scriveste, scrissero*
Spegnere:	*Spensi, spegnesti, spense, spegnemmo, spegneste, spensero*
Stare:	*Stetti, stesti, stette, stemmo, steste, stettero*
Tenere:	*Tenni, tenesti, tenne, tenemmo, teneste, tennero*
Vedere:	*Vidi, vedesti, vide, vedemmo, vedeste, videro*
Venire:	*Venni, venisti, venne, venimmo, veniste, vennero*
Vincere:	*Vinsi, vincesti, vinse, vincemmo, vinceste, vinsero*
Vivere:	*Vissi, vivesti, visse, vivemmo, viveste, vissero*
Volere:	*Volli, volesti, volle, volemmo, voleste, vollero*

11. Practice

Write the *passato remoto* of the verbs in the person indicated.

Io:

chiedere

conoscere

sentire

_____   _____   _____

Tu:

comprare

temere

finire

_____   _____   _____

Carlo:

nascere

vedere

volere

_____   _____   _____

Maria:

capire

scrivere

venire

_____   _____   _____

Noi:

fare

bere

ridere

_____   _____   _____

Voi:

scendere

vincere

mettere

_____   _____   _____

Loro:

offrire

partire

fare

_____   _____   _____

12. Practice

Rewrite in English.

1. Io venni _____
2. Io risi _____
3. Io bevvi _____
4. Lui cadde _____
5. Lei chiese _____
6. Noi chiudemmo _____
7. Voi conosceste _____
8. Tu dicesti _____
9. Lei decise _____
10. Noi dicemmo _____
11. Voi doveste _____
12. Loro dissero _____
13. Io vissi _____
14. Loro vinsero _____
15. Tu facesti _____
16. Lei lesse _____
17. Noi leggemmo _____
18. Tu mettesti _____
19. Voi nasceste _____
20. Io presi _____

21. Noi prendemmo _____
22. Tu ridesti _____
23. Loro risero _____
24. Lei rimase _____
25. Tu scegliesti _____
26. Loro scrissero _____
27. Io scelsi _____
28. Tu scegliesti _____
29. Loro scrissero _____
30. Voi steste _____
31. Tu vedesti _____
32. Noi vedemmo _____
33. Voi vinceste _____
34. Io vidi _____
35. Loro videro _____
36. Lei visse _____
37. Lui volle _____
38. Noi volemmo _____
39. Loro vennero _____
40. Tu stesti _____

13. Review Practice

Practices 13 and 14 review the *present, imperative, imperfect, future,* and *passato remoto.*
Rewrite in English.

1. Parlo _____

2. Mangiamo _____

3. Abitano _____

4. Abitate? _____

5. Guidiamo _____

6. Non lavoro _____

7. Ritorneremo _____

8. Ritorneranno _____

9. Non volo _____

10. Volate? _____

11. Arriveranno _____

12. Arriverò _____

13. Non arriverete _____

14. Chiedo _____

15. Non chiedevo _____

16. Chiudono _____

17. Chiudi? _____

18. Penso _____

19. Penserai _____

20. Riposiamo _____

21. Riposano _____

22. Non riposi _____

23. Parlai _____

24. Pensammo _____

25. Riposi? _____

26. Mangia! _____

27. Guardate! _____

28. Parlate! _____

29. Impara! _____

30. Non guardare! _____

31. Non dormire! _____

32. Senta! _____

33. Prometti? _____

34. Risponderò _____

35. Scriveremo _____

36. Leggevo _____

37. Parlavi _____

38. Volevate _____

39. Piangevano _____

40. Insistevi _____

41. Bevevi _____

42. Bevi! _____

43. Bevete! _____

44. Non bere! _____

45. Vieni _____

46. Vieni? _____

47. Lesse _____

48. Sentiste _____

14. Review Practice

Rewrite in Italian.

1. They live _____
2. I used to open _____
3. They worked _____
4. We climb _____
5. I understand _____
6. They ate _____
7. We ate _____
8. He works _____
9. They study _____
10. I keep _____
11. I write _____
12. You (s.) used to write _____
13. I'll write _____
14. You (s.) travel _____
15. You (s.) used to travel _____
16. They'll travel _____
17. I leave _____
18. He leaves _____
19. We'll leave _____
20. She was leaving _____
21. He was learning _____
22. We were learning _____
23. They thought _____

24. I'll live _____
25. We'll open _____
26. Eat (s.)! _____
27. Work (s.)! _____
28. He'll eat _____
29. He'll work _____
30. Study (s.)! _____
31. Study (pl.)! _____
32. Drink (s.)! _____
33. Drink (pl.)! _____
34. We promised _____
35. I wanted _____
36. She must _____
37. Answer (s.)! _____
38. Write (s.) (formal)! _____
39. Speak (s.) (formal)! _____
40. I said _____
41. We'll wait _____
42. I discuss _____
43. We used to see _____
44. They know _____
45. We understand _____
46. I used to think _____

Chapter 5

Essere (to Be) and *Avere* (to Have)

1. Forms of *Essere* and *Avere*

It is important to become familiar with the irregular verbs **essere** and **avere,** two of the most commonly used verbs in Italian. Besides being used alone in the usual conjugations, they are also used to form the compound tenses.

Following are the complete conjugations of **essere** and **avere.** (Note that some of the tenses will be covered in later chapters.)

Essere

Avere

Present Indicative

sono, sei, è, siamo, siete, sono

ho, hai, ha, abbiamo, avete, hanno

Imperfect

ero, eri, era, eravamo,
eravate, erano

avevo, avevi, aveva, avevamo,
avevate, avevano

Future

sarò, sarai, sarà, saremo,
sarete, saranno

avrò, avrai, avrà, avremo,
avrete, avranno

Imperative

sii, siamo, siate
sia (pol. s.), siano (pol. pl.)

abbi, abbiamo, abbiate
abbia (pol. s.), abbiano (pol. pl.)

Passato Remoto (Preterit)

fui, fosti, fu, fummo
foste, furono

ebbi, avesti, ebbe, avemmo,
aveste, ebbero

Passato Prossimo (Present Perfect)

sono stato/a, sei stato/a, è stato/a,
siamo stati/e, siete stati/e, sono stati/e

ho avuto, hai avuto, ha avuto,
abbiamo avuto, avete avuto,
hanno avuto

Trapassato Prossimo (Pluperfect)

ero stato/a, eri stato/a, era stato/a,
eravamo stati/e, eravate stati/e,
erano stati/e

avevo avuto, avevi avuto, aveva
avuto, avevamo avuto, avevate
avuto, avevano avuto

Essere	*Avere*

Essere

Present Conditional
sarei, saresti, sarebbe, saremmo,
sareste, sarebbero

Past Conditional
sarei stato/a, saresti stato/a, sarebbe
stato/a, saremmo stati/e, sareste stati/e,
sarebbero stati/e

Present Subjunctive
che io sia, tu sia, lui/lei sia,
noi siamo, voi siate, loro siano

Imperfect Subjunctive
che io fossi, tu fossi,
lui/lei fosse,
noi fossimo, voi foste,
loro fossero

Past Subjunctive
che io sia stato/a, tu sia
stato/a, lui/lei sia stato/a,
noi siano stati/e, voi siate
stati/e, loro siano stati/e

Pluperfect Subjunctive
che io fossi stato/a, tu fossi stato/a,
lui/lei fosse stato/a,
noi fossimo stati/e, voi foste
stati/e, loro fossero stati/e

Avere

avrei, avresti, avrebbe, avremmo,
avreste, avrebbero

avrei avuto, avresti avuto,
avrebbe, avuto, avremmo avuto,
avreste avuto, avrebbero avuto

che io abbia, tu abbia, lui/lei
abbia, noi abbiamo, voi abbiate,
loro abbiano

che io avessi, tu avessi,
lui/lei avesse,
noi avessimo, voi aveste,
loro avessero

che io abbia avuto, tu abbia
avuto, lui/lei abbia avuto,
noi abbiamo avuto, voi abbiate
avuto, loro abbiano avuto

che io avessi avuto, tu avessi
avuto, lui/lei avesse avuto,
noi avessimo avuto, voi aveste
avuto, loro avessero avuto

Passato Prossimo with *Avere*

2. Uses of the Passato Prossimo

The *passato prossimo* (present perfect) is used to describe actions and events that occurred in the recent past. It is often preceded or followed by such time expressions as *ieri, domenica scorsa, l'anno scorso, un anno fa, un'ora fa.*

3. Forms of the Passato Prossimo with *Avere*

The *passato prossimo* of most Italian verbs is formed by the present tense of the auxiliary verb *avere* and the past participle of the verb.

Examples:			
	io	*ho mangiato*	I have eaten
	tu	*hai mangiato*	you have eaten
	lui	*ha mangiato*	he has eaten
	lei	*ha mangiato*	she has eaten
	noi	*abbiamo mangiato*	we have eaten
	voi	*avete mangiato*	you have eaten
	loro	*hanno mangiato*	they have eaten

The *past participle* is formed, for regular verbs, by adding:

> *ato* to the infinitive root of *-are* verbs
> *uto* to the infinitive root of *-ere* verbs
> *ito* to the infinitive root of *-ire* verbs

Infinitive:	*parlare* (to speak)	*vedere* (to see)	*sentire* (to hear)
Past Participle:	*parlato* (spoken)	*veduto* (seen)	*sentito* (heard)

In English, the *passato prossimo* is translated either with the simple past or the present perfect.

Examples:	*Ho mangiato* alle otto.	I *ate* at eight o'clock.
	Ho mangiato tardi.	I *have* eaten late.

Note: With the verb *avere,* the past participle doesn't agree in gender and number with the subject. The negative is formed by placing *non* in front of *avere.* If there is a second negative, this follows *avere.*

Examples:	*Non ho parlato* molto.	I didn't talk a lot.
	Non ho mai parlato molto.	I never talked a lot.

Passato Prossimo with *Essere*

4. Forms of the Passato Prossimo with *Essere*

The *passato prossimo* of several Italian verbs is formed with the auxiliary verb *essere* plus the past participle. The past participle agrees in gender and in number with the subject.

Examples:	Masculine		Feminine	
	io	*sono andato*	*io*	*sono andata*
	tu	*sei andato*	*tu*	*sei andata*
	lui	*è andato*	*lei*	*è andata*
	noi	*siamo andati*	*noi*	*siamo andate*
	voi	*siete andati*	*voi*	*siete andate*
	loro	*sono andati*	*loro*	*sono andate*

5. Common Verbs with *Essere* in the Passato Prossimo

Following is a list of commonly used verbs that form the *passato prossimo* with *essere*.

accadere	to happen	*E' accaduto un incidente.*	An accident happened.
andare	to go	*Sono andato/a a scuola.*	I went to school.
arrivare	to arrive	*È arrivata tardi.*	She arrived late.
diventare	to become	*È diventato famoso.*	He became famous.
entrare	to enter	*Sono entrato/a.*	I went inside.
morire	to die	*Il cane è morto.*	The dog died.
nascere	to be born	*Sono nati/e ieri.*	They were born yesterday.
partire	to depart	*Gianni è già partito.*	John left already.
restare	to remain	*Lei è restata a casa.*	She remained at home.
rimanere	to remain	*Lui è rimasto a casa.*	He remained at home.
scendere	to descend	*Siamo scesi/e in fretta.*	We descended in a hurry.
stare	to stay	*Sono state a casa.*	They stayed home.
tornare	to return	*Siete tornati tardi.*	You returned late.
uscire	to go out	*È appena uscito.*	He just went out.
venire	to come	*Sono venuto/a in America.*	I came to America.

Irregular Past Participles

6. List of Irregular Past Participles

Many Italian verbs, especially *-ere* verbs, have irregular past participles.

Following is a list of the most common verbs with irregular *past participles:*

Infinitive		Past Participle
accendere	to turn on	*acceso*
aggiungere	to add	*aggiunto*
apparire	to appear	*apparso*
appendere	to hang	*appeso*
apprendere	to learn	*appreso*
aprire	to open	*aperto*
assumere	to hire	*assunto*
bere	to drink	*bevuto*
chiedere	to ask	*chiesto*
chiudere	to close	*chiuso*
cogliere	to gather	*colto*
comprendere	to comprehend	*compreso*
concludere	to conclude	*concluso*
confondere	to confuse	*confuso*
conoscere	to know	*conosciuto*
convincere	to convince	*convinto*
coprire	to cover	*coperto*
correre	to run	*corso*
correggere	to correct	*corretto*
cuocere	to cook	*cotto*
decidere	to decide	*deciso*
difendere	to defend	*difeso*
dire	to tell, say	*detto*
discutere	to discuss	*discusso*
distinguere	to distinguish	*distinto*
dividere	to divide	*diviso*
eleggere	to elect	*eletto*
esprimere	to express	*espresso*
fare	to make, do	*fatto*
includere	to include	*incluso*
interrompere	to interrupt	*interrotto*
leggere	to read	*letto*

Infinitive		Past Participle
mettere	to put	*messo*
morire	to die	*morto*
muovere	to move	*mosso*
nascere	to be born	*nato*
nascondere	to hide	*nascosto*
offrire	to offer	*offerto*
perdere	to lose	*perso*
permettere	to permit	*permesso*
prendere	to take, get	*preso*
promettere	to promise	*promesso*
promuovere	to promote	*promosso*
proporre	to propose	*proposto*
porre	to put	*posto*
proteggere	to protect	*protetto*
provvedere	to provide	*provvisto*
raggiungere	to reach	*raggiunto*
richiedere	to request	*richiesto*
ridere	to laugh	*riso*
ridurre	to reduce	*ridotto*
rimanere	to remain	*rimasto*
rimuovere	to remove	*rimosso*
risolvere	to resolve	*risolto*
rispondere	to answer	*risposto*
rompere	to break	*rotto*
scegliere	to choose	*scelto*
scendere	to descend	*sceso*
scomparire	to disappear	*scomparso*
scrivere	to write	*scritto*
soffrire	to suffer	*sofferto*
sorridere	to smile	*sorriso*
spegnere	to turn off	*spento*
spendere	to spend	*speso*
spingere	to push	*spinto*
succedere	to happen	*successo*
togliere	to remove	*tolto*
trasmettere	to broadcast	*trasmesso*
vedere	to see	*visto*
vincere	to win	*vinto*
vivere	to live	*vissuto*

7. Practice

Write the *passato prossimo* of the verbs.

1. **mangiare**   io _____   tu _____   lui, lei _____

    (to eat)   noi _____   voi _____   loro _____

2. **scrivere**   io _____   tu _____   lui, lei _____

    (to write)   noi _____   voi _____   loro _____

3. **venire**   io _____   tu _____   lui, lei _____

    (to come)   noi _____   voi _____   loro _____

4. **andare**   io _____   tu _____   lui, lei _____

    (to go)   noi _____   voi _____   loro _____

8. Practice

Write the verb in the *passato prossimo* in the person indicated.

Io:

mangiare   vedere   sentire

_____   _____   _____

Tu:

parlare   scrivere   capire

_____   _____   _____

Lui:

viaggiare   potere   finire

_____   _____   _____

Lei:

camminare   volere   venire

_____   _____   _____

Noi:

lodare   spingere   salire

_____   _____   _____

Voi:

stare   ridere   aprire

_____   _____   _____

Loro:

dare   rimanere   nutrire

_____   _____   _____

Carlo:

fare   nascere   offrire

_____   _____   _____

Maria:

andare   nascondere   pulire

_____   _____   _____

Io e Giovanni:

aspettare   vendere   partire

_____   _____   _____

Tu e Pietro:

imparare   chiudere   uscire

_____   _____   _____

Giovanni e Paolo:

fermare   vivere   finire

_____   _____   _____

9. Practice

Write the verbs in the *passato prossimo*, using the negative in the person indicated.

Io:

essere   avere   potere

_____   _____   _____

Tu:

volere   dovere   capire

_____   _____   _____

Lui:

fare   dare   stare

_____   _____   _____

Noi:

andare   arrivare   partire

_____   _____   _____

10. Practice

Write the verbs in the *passato prossimo* in the person indicated by the subject.

1. Lui (parlare) _____
2. Noi (stare)_____
3. Lei (stare) _____
4. Voi (leggere)_____
5. Loro (sentire) _____
6. Io (dormire)_____
7. Tu (perdere) _____
8. Lei (andare)_____
9. Lui (decidere) _____
10. Noi (comprare)_____
11. Voi (vivere) _____
12. Loro (bere) _____
13. Lui (parlare) _____
14. Lei (aprire) _____
15. Lui (aprire) _____
16. Voi (imparare) _____
17. Noi (temere) _____
18. Io (mangiare) _____
19. Tu (ricevere)_____
20. Lui (lavorare) _____
21. Noi (viaggiare) _____
22. Loro (potere)_____
23. Voi (insegnare)_____
24. Noi (sciare)_____
25. Noi (correre)_____
26. Io (guardare)_____
27. Tu (guarire)_____
28. Voi (rispondere) _____
29. Loro (arrivare) _____
30. Noi (tenere) _____
31. Lei (vendere) _____
32. Loro (vivere) _____
33. Io (abitare) _____
34. Noi (gettare) _____

11. Practice

Write the verbs in the *passato prossimo,* using the negative in the person indicated.

1. Lui (mangiare) _____
2. Lei (comprare) _____
3. Tu (parlare)_____
4. Io (studiare) _____
5. Loro (dovere) _____
6. Noi (cantare)_____
7. Loro (vedere) _____
8. Voi (sentire) _____
9. Tu (scrivere) _____
10. Noi (volere) _____

12. Practice

Rewrite in Italian, using the *passato prossimo.*

1. We answered _____
2. They bought _____
3. We learned _____
4. She bought _____
5. I asked _____
6. You (s.) answered _____
7. We left _____
8. I drank _____
9. I didn't drink _____
10. They taught _____
11. I read_____
12. You (s.) wrote _____
13. They worked _____
14. He slept _____
15. She worked _____
16. We studied _____
17. He didn't ski _____
18. She didn't go _____
19. She was born _____

20. They sold _____
21. I didn't listen _____
22. I didn't hear _____
23. I didn't ask_____
24. You (s.) didn't answer_____
25. I received _____
26. I learned _____
27. They understood_____
28. She traveled _____
29. We didn't travel_____
30. They cleaned _____
31. We thought _____
32. They didn't think _____
33. I cleaned _____
34. You (s.) paid _____
35. You (s.) didn't pay_____
36. We ate_____
37. I arrived _____
38. They stayed _____

Trapassato Prossimo

13. Forms of the Trapassato Prossimo

The *trapassato prossimo* (pluperfect) is formed by using the imperfect of the auxiliary verbs *avere* or *essere,* plus the *past participle.*

Examples:				
avevo mangiato	I had eaten	*ero andato/a*	I had gone
avevi mangiato	you had eaten	*eri andato/a*	you had gone
aveva mangiato	he had eaten	*era andato*	he had gone
aveva mangiato	she had eaten	*era andata*	she had gone
avevamo mangiato	we had eaten	*eravamo andati/e*	we had gone
avevate mangiato	you had eaten	*eravate andati/e*	you had gone
avevano mangiato	they had eaten	*erano andati/e*	they had gone

14. Uses of the Trapassato Prossimo

This tense is used to express an action in the past that had happened before another one. The more recent past action can be expressed in the *passato prossimo, passato remoto,* or *imperfect.*

Examples:	Dove è stato Giulio?	Where did Giulio go?
	È andato in vacanza	He went on vacation
	dove *era stato* tanti	where he had been
	anni fa.	many years ago.

15. Practice

Write the *trapassato prossimo* of the verbs.

1. **guardare**   io _____   tu _____   lui, lei _____

   (to look)   noi _____   voi _____   loro _____

2. **vedere**   io _____   tu _____   lui, lei _____

   (to see)   noi _____   voi _____   loro _____

3. **partire**   io _____   tu _____   lui, lei _____

   (to leave)   noi _____   voi _____   loro _____

16. Practice

Write the verbs in the *trapassato prossimo* in the person indicated.

Io:

mangiare   vedere   sentire

_____   _____   _____

Tu:

parlare   credere   pulire

_____   _____   _____

Lui, Lei:

visitare   scrivere   finire

_____   _____   _____

Noi:

arrivare   bere   capire

_____   _____   _____

Voi:

comprare   leggere   venire

_____   _____   _____

Loro:

dare   potere   aprire

_____   _____   _____

Carlo:

giocare   spingere   costruire

_____   _____   _____

Carlo e Maria:

viaggiare   vendere   partire

_____   _____   _____

17. Practice

Rewrite in Italian, using the *trapassato prossimo*.

1. I had understood _____
2. You had gone _____
3. She had studied _____
4. He had drunk _____
5. We had finished _____
6. You (pl.) had slept _____
7. They had bought _____
8. I had worked _____
9. You (s.) had thought _____
10. He had played _____
11. We had traveled _____
12. You (pl.) had cleaned _____
13. They had watched _____
14. I had been _____
15. You (s.) had arrived _____
16. He had left _____
17. She had gone _____
18. We had read _____
19. You (pl.) had written _____
20. They had finished _____
21. I had won _____
22. He had lost _____
23. She had gone _____
24. We had listened _____

18. Review Practice

This practice reviews the *passato prossimo* and *trapassato prossimo*.

Rewrite in Italian.

1. I have eaten _____

2. You (s.) had eaten _____

3. She has gone _____

4. He had come _____

5. We have finished _____

6. We had finished _____

7. You (pl.) have seen _____

8. You (pl.) had looked _____

9. They have read _____

10. They had read _____

11. I have played _____

12. I had slept _____

13. He has eaten _____

14. We had skied _____

15. We have not read _____

16. We had not thought _____

17. They have not won _____

18. They had not promised _____

19. I have not chosen _____

20. He has not come _____

21. She had not left _____

22. We have lived _____

23. We have not lived _____

24. We had lived _____

Chapter 6

Conditional

1. Uses of the Conditional

The conditional *(condizionale)* is used to refer to an action or state that **may** happen if something else occurred or if some condition were present. In English, the conditional is indicated by **would**.

>**Example:** Al tuo posto **studierei** di più.   In your place I would study more.

The conditional is used to add politeness or kindness to wishes and demands.

>**Examples:** **Vorrei** un caffè.   I would like a coffee.
>   Mi **faresti** un favore?   Would you do me a favor?

2. Forms of the Conditional

The **present conditional** tense is made up of the future root plus the conditional endings, which are the same for all three conjugations.

Cantare (To sing)	**Vendere** (To sell)	**Sentire** (To hear)
io canter**ei**	vender**ei**	sentir**ei**
tu canter**esti**	vender**esti**	sentir**esti**
lui canter**ebbe**	vender**ebbe**	sentir**ebbe**
lei canter**ebbe**	vender**ebbe**	sentir**ebbe**
noi canter**emmo**	vender**emmo**	sentir**emmo**
voi canter**este**	vender**este**	sentir**este**
loro canter**ebbero**	vender**ebbero**	sentir**ebbero**

Note: Remember the use of *e* in the stem for *-are* verbs.

Verbs ending in *-care* and *-gare* add an *h* in the conditional to keep the hard *c* and *g* sounds: *pagherei, giocherei.*

Verbs ending in *-ciare* and *-giare* drop the *i* in the conditional: *comincerei, mangerei.*

Verbs that have irregular roots in the future use the same irregular roots in the conditional. Following are the most common verbs that have irregular roots:

andare	*andr*	*andrei, andresti, etc.*
bere	*berr*	*berrei, berresti, etc.*
cadere	*cadr*	*cadrei, cadresti, etc.*
dare	*dar*	*darei, daresti, etc.*
dovere	*dovr*	*dovrei, dovresti, etc.*
essere	*sar*	*sarei, saresti, etc.*
fare	*far*	*farei, faresti, etc.*
potere	*potr*	*potrei, potresti, etc.*
sapere	*sapr*	*saprei, sapresti, etc.*
valere	*varr*	*varrei, varresti, etc.*
vedere	*vedr*	*vedrei, vedresti, etc.*
venire	*verr*	*verrei, verresti, etc.*
volere	*vorr*	*vorrei, vorresti, etc.*

Note: The conditional of *dovere* is translated as **should.**

3. Practice

Write the *present conditional* of the verbs.

1. **andare**   io _____   tu _____   lui, lei _____
   (to go)   noi _____   voi _____   loro _____

2. **dovere**   io _____   tu _____   lui, lei _____
   (to have to, must) noi _____ voi _____ loro _____

3. **venire**   io _____   tu _____   lui, lei _____
   (to come)   noi _____   voi _____   loro _____

4. Practice

Write the verbs in the *present conditional* in the person indicated.

Io:

cantare   potere   capire

_____   _____   _____

Tu:

ballare   vedere   dormire

_____   _____   _____

Lui, Lei:

nuotare   bere   sentire

_____   _____   _____

Noi:

ordinare   leggere   finire

_____   _____   _____

Voi:

viaggiare   dovere   partire

_____   _____   _____

Loro:

domandare   volere   venire

_____   _____   _____

Giovanna:

ascoltare   avere   dire

_____   _____   _____

Io e Carlo:

parlare   vedere   colpire

_____   _____   _____

Tu e Giovanna:

desiderare   vincere   ubbidire

_____   _____   _____

Giovanna e Carlo:

organizzare   promettere   offrire

_____   _____   _____

_____

5. Practice

Write the verbs in the *negative* of the *present conditional.*

Io:

parlare   vedere   sentire

_____   _____   _____

Tu:

viaggiare   scrivere   pulire

_____   _____   _____

Paolo:

mangiare   potere   capire

_____   _____   _____

Io e Carlo:

studiare   leggere   finire

_____   _____   _____

Tu e Paolo:

arrivare   volere   partire

_____   _____   _____

6. Practice

Rewrite in English.

1. Comprerei _____

2. Vedresti _____

3. Capirei _____

4. Non mangeremmo _____

5. Verreste _____

6. Sentirebbero _____

7. Studierei _____

8. Non studierei _____

9. Viaggeresti _____

10. Capirebbe _____

11. Carla arriverebbe _____

12. Saremmo _____

13. Scriverebbero _____

14. Dormirei _____

15. Non leggeresti _____

16. Paolo non partirebbe _____

17. Faremmo _____

18. Non giochereste _____

19. Sareste _____

20. Ascolterebbero _____

21. Verrei _____

22. Non verrei _____

23. Staresti _____

24. Carlo capirebbe _____

25. Maria cucinerebbe _____

26. Giocheremmo _____

27. Vorremmo _____

28. Non vorremmo _____

29. Tu e Paolo fareste _____

30. Non farei _____

31. Andremmo _____

32. Portereste _____

33. Carla non porterebbe _____

34. Dovrebbero _____

35. Inviterei _____

36. Verrebbero _____

Interrogative Forms

1. Verresti? _____

2. Canterebbero? _____

3. Capirebbe? _____

4. Dareste? _____

5. Parlerebbe? _____

6. Sentiresti? _____

7. Faremmo? _____

8. Cucineresti? _____

7. Practice

Rewrite in Italian, using the *present conditional.*

1. I would think _____
2. I would drink _____
3. You could _____
4. He would do_____
5. He would not do _____
6. She would write_____
7. I would work _____
8. They would drink _____
9. I would clean _____
10. She would make _____
11. They would wash_____
12. I would watch _____
13. They would see _____
14. We would think _____
15. I would wash _____
16. You (s.) would understand _____
17. They would not go_____
18. You (pl.) would see _____
19. I would not take_____
20. I would know_____

21. You (s.) would go _____
22. You (s.) could not _____
23. She would think_____
24. We would write _____
25. They would read _____
26. I would sleep _____
27. They could not_____
28. We would eat_____
29. I would drink _____
30. You (pl.) would travel_____
31. She would return _____
32. He would arrive _____
33. They would leave_____
34. I would not arrive _____
35. She would not plant_____
36. He would win _____
37. They would eat _____
38. We would swim _____
39. You (pl.) would ski _____
40. We would look _____

8. Practice

Rewrite in Italian. Use the conditional of *dovere.*

1. I should go _____
2. You (s.) should write_____
3. They should study _____

4. We should come _____
5. He should cook _____
6. She should read _____

Past Conditional

9. Forms of the Past Conditional

The *past conditional (condizionale passato)* is a compound tense. It is formed by the conditional tense of the auxiliary *avere* or *essere* plus the past participle of the main verb. The past participle agrees with the subject when the verb is conjugated with the auxiliary *essere.*

10. Uses of the Past Conditional

The *past conditional* is used in dependent clauses to express an action that is considered future as viewed from the past. In English the present conditional is used, but in Italian the past conditional is used.

>   **Example:**   Ha detto che *avrebbe scritto.*   He said that he would write (he would have written).

The *condizionale passato* of *dovere* followed by an infinitive expresses an obligation that was not done.

>   **Example:**   *Avresti dovuto scrivere*   You should have written
>   a tua mamma.   to your mother.

The *condizionale passato* is also used in sentences with *se* clauses. These will be studied in the next chapter.

11. Practice

Write the *past conditional* of the verbs.

1. **parlare**   io _____   tu _____   lui, lei _____
    (to speak)   noi _____   voi _____   loro _____

2. **vedere**   io _____   tu _____   lui, lei _____
    (to see)   noi _____   voi _____   loro _____

3. **venire**   io _____   tu _____   lui, lei _____
    (to come)   noi _____   voi _____   loro _____

12. Practice

Write the verbs in the *past conditional* in the person indicated.

Io:

andare	ritornare	partire
_____	_____	_____

Tu:

parlare	vedere	capire
_____	_____	_____

Lui, Lei:

arrivare	scrivere	dormire
_____	_____	_____

Noi:

informare	leggere	preferire
_____	_____	_____

Voi:

aspettare	dovere	finire
_____	_____	_____

Loro:

abitare	bere	uscire
_____	_____	_____

Carlo:

invitare	volere	sentire
_____	_____	_____

13. Review Practice

Practices 13 and 14 review the *present conditional* and the *past conditional.*
Rewrite in English.

1. Io avrei aspettato _____

2. Tu parleresti _____

3. Avrebbe mangiato _____

4. Capirebbero _____

5. Scrivereste _____

6. Avreste scritto _____

7. Risponderebbero _____

8. Non avrebbe risposto _____

9. Sentirei _____

10. Avrei sentito _____

11. Avremmo firmato _____

12. Inviterei _____

13. Uscireste _____

14. Finiremmo _____

15. Avrebbero finito _____

16. Comprereste _____

17. (Lui) comprerebbe _____

18. Troveresti _____

19. Avrei guardato _____

20. Risponderebbe _____

21. Avrebbe risposto _____

22. Avreste scritto _____

23. Saprei _____

24. Avrebbe saputo _____

14. Review Practice

Rewrite in Italian.

1. I would go   _____

2. You (s.) would have taken   _____

3. We would have danced   _____

4. They would have come   _____

5. She would know   _____

6. We would wait   _____

7. We would have started   _____

8. She would write   _____

9. He would have answered   _____

10. They would speak   _____

11. They should have come   _____

12. I should have spoken   _____

13. She should wait   _____

14. She should have waited   _____

15. We would understand   _____

16. They would have understood   _____

17. She would have written   _____

18. You (s.) would have answered   _____

19. You (s.) should have answered   _____

20. They would travel   _____

21. I would have returned   _____

22. He would have left   _____

23. She would arrive   _____

24. We would leave   _____

Chapter 7

Present Subjunctive

1. Uses of the Subjunctive

The subjunctive *(congiuntivo)* is used very frequently in Italian, while in English it is used very rarely. In Italian, the subjunctive is generally used in a dependent *che* clause and reflects the wishes, hopes, emotions, opinions, feelings, and doubts of the subject.

It is used mainly after the following verbs: *pensare, credere, sperare, dubitare, non sapere, avere paura, volere.* The verb in the main clause is in the indicative, and the *che* clause is in the subjunctive.

Examples:	Spero *che tu venga.*	I hope that you come.
	Vogliono *che io venga.*	They want me to come.

If there is no change of subject, the infinitive is used instead of the subjunctive after the verbs. The preposition *di* is used with certain verbs such as *sperare, avere voglia, avere paura.*

Examples:	*Ho voglia di andare.*	I have a desire to go.
	Spero di vederlo.	I hope to see him/it.

2. Forms of the Present Subjunctive

The *present subjunctive* is formed by putting the endings of the subjunctive on the infinitive root. Following are the conjugations of the present subjunctive of regular *-are, -ere, -ire* verbs.

Che + pronoun	Parlare	Vedere	Sentire
che io	parl*i*	ved*a*	sent*a*
che tu	parl*i*	ved*a*	sent*a*
che lui	parl*i*	ved*a*	sent*a*
che lei	parl*i*	ved*a*	sent*a*
che noi	parl*iamo*	ved*iamo*	sent*iamo*
che voi	parl*iate*	ved*iate*	sent*iate*
che loro	parl*ino*	ved*ano*	sent*ano*

It is important in this tense to use the personal pronouns for the first three persons if the subject is unclear.

Example:	Penso *che lui capisca.*	I think that he understands.

The verbs in *-care* and *-gare* add an *h* in all forms of the present subjunctive.

Examples:

Giocare (To play)	**Pagare** (To pay)
che io gio*chi*	che io pag*hi*
che tu gio*chi*	che io pag*hi*
che lui gio*chi*	che lui pag*hi*
che lei gio*chi*	che lei pag*hi*
che noi gio*chiamo*	che noi pag*hiamo*
che voi gio*chiate*	che voi pag*hiate*
che loro gio*chino*	che loro pag*hino*

The verbs in *-ciare* and *-giare* do not repeat the *i.*

Examples:

Cominciare (To begin, start)	**Mangiare** (To eat)
che io cominc*i*	che io mang*i*
che tu cominc*i*	che tu mang*i*
che lui cominc*i*	che lui mang*i*
che lei cominc*i*	che lei mang*i*
che noi cominc*iamo*	che noi mang*iamo*
che voi cominc*iate*	che voi mang*iate*
che loro cominc*ino*	che loro mang*ino*

Verbs of the *-ire* conjugation with *isc* add an *-isc* between the root and the ending in all the singular persons and the 3rd person plural.

Example:

Che + pronoun	**Finire** (to finish)
che io	fin*isca*
che tu	fin*isca*
che lui	fin*isca*
che lei	fin*isca*
che noi	fin*iamo*
che voi	fin*iate*
che loro	fin*iscano*

The following commonly used verbs have irregular forms in the ***present subjunctive.*** All the endings have the vowel ***a*** regardless of whether they are ***-are, -ere,*** or ***-ire*** verbs.

andare	*vada, vada, vada, andiamo, andiate, vadano*
avere	*abbia, abbia, abbia, abbiamo, abbiate, abbiano*
bere	*beva, beva, beva, beviamo, beviate, bevano*
dare	*dia, dia, dia, diamo, diate, diano*
dire	*dica, dica, dica, diciamo, diciate, dicano*
dovere	*debba, debba, debba, dobbiamo, dobbiate, debbano*
essere	*sia, sia, sia, siamo, siate, siano*
fare	*faccia, faccia, faccia, facciamo, facciate, facciano*
potere	*possa, possa, possa, possiamo, possiate, possano*
rimanere	*rimanga, rimanga, rimanga, rimaniamo, rimaniate, rimangano*
sapere	*sappia, sappia, sappia, sappiamo, sappiate, sappiano*
stare	*stia, stia, stia, stiamo, stiate, stiano*
uscire	*esca, esca, esca, usciamo, usciate, escano*
venire	*venga, venga, venga, veniamo, veniate, vengano*
volere	*voglia, voglia, voglia, vogliamo, vogliate, vogliano*

3. The Subjunctive after Impersonal Expressions

The ***present subjunctive*** is used in a dependent ***che*** clause after impersonal expressions of possibility, opinion, and probability.

> **Example:**   ***È necessario che tu venga.***   It is necessary that you come.

Here are some impersonal expressions with which the subjunctive is used:

È necessario	It is necessary
È probabile	It is probable
È opportuno	It is opportune
È improbabile	It is improbable
È bene	It is good
È meglio	It is better
È giusto	It is right
È importante	It is important
È preferibile	It is preferable

If the impersonal verb indicates certainty, the subjunctive is not used.

> **Example:**   ***È certo che vengono oggi.***   It is certain they are coming today.

The impersonal expressions can also be followed by the infinitive with no subject indicated.

> **Example:**   ***È necessario studiare.***   It is necessary to study.

4. Practice

1. **domandare**   che io _____   che tu _____   che lui, lei _____
   (to ask)   che noi _____   che voi _____   che loro _____

2. **vedere**   che io _____   che tu _____   che lui, lei _____
   (to see)   che noi _____   che voi _____   che loro _____

3. **sentire**   che io _____   che tu _____   che lui, lei _____
   (to hear)   che noi _____   che voi _____   che loro _____

4. **capire**   che io _____   che tu _____   che lui, lei _____
   (to understand)   che noi _____   che voi _____   che loro _____

5. **giocare**   che io _____   che tu _____   che lui, lei _____
   (to play)   che noi _____   che voi _____   che loro _____

6. **pagare**   che io _____   che tu _____   che lui, lei _____
   (to pay)   che noi _____   che voi _____   che loro _____

5. Practice

Write the verbs in the *present subjunctive* in the person indicated.

Che io:

domandare

_____

decidere

_____

sentire

_____

Che tu:

comprare

_____

vedere

_____

finire

_____

Che lui:

preparare

_____

leggere

_____

capire

_____

Che lei:

aspettare

_____

comprendere

_____

pulire

_____

Che noi:

arrivare

_____

accendere

_____

dire

_____

Che voi:

visitare

_____

bere

_____

partire

_____

Che loro:

lavorare

_____

chiudere

_____

capire

_____

6. Practice

Write the verbs in the *present subjunctive* in the person indicated or in the *infinitive.*

Io voglio che tu:

mangiare   leggere   partire

_____   _____   _____

Io voglio che lui:

parlare   perdere   offrire

_____   _____   _____

Io voglio che lei:

stare   discutere   aprire

_____   _____   _____

Io spero che noi:

imparare   sorridere   capire

_____   _____   _____

Io desidero che voi:

fare   vedere   ridere

_____   _____   _____

Io penso che loro:

desiderare   dovere   ubbidire

_____   _____   _____

Io voglio:

visitare   vincere   capire

_____   _____   _____

Loro vogliono:

visitare   arrivare   partire

_____   _____   _____

7. Practice

Choose the correct form of the verb from those in parentheses.

1. Mio padre vuole che io (legga, leggo) _____

2. Speriamo che i ragazzi (studiano, studino) _____

3. Spero che loro (comprano, comprino) _____

4. Penso che lui (capisce, capisca) _____

5. È necessario che io (vengo, venga) _____

6. È possibile che loro (arrivano, arrivino) _____

7. Vuole che tu (finisci, finisca) _____

8. Voglio che tu (vieni, venga) _____

9. Penso che tu (puoi, possa) _____

10. Credo che lui (legge, legga) _____

11. È bene che noi (veniamo, venire) _____

12. È possibile che voi (pensate, pensiate) _____

13. Credo di (sapere, sappia) _____

14. Spera che io (ritorni, ritorno) _____

15. Dubito che tu (sappia, so) _____

16. È bene che io (vado, vada) _____

17. Dubitiamo che lui (vince, vinca) _____

18. È possibile che lui (perda, perde) _____

19. È importante che loro (pensino, pensano) _____

20. È giusto che io (controlli, controllo) _____

21. È possibile che loro (possono, possano) _____

22. Ho voglia di (sapere, so) _____

23. Spero che loro (puliscano, puliscono) _____

24. Spera di (comprare, compri) _____

8. Practice

Change the verb from the *present indicative* to the *present subjunctive.*

1. Vado   _____
2. Sente (lui)   _____
3. Mangiamo   _____
4. Parlano   _____
5. Sentite   _____
6. Bevi   _____
7. Parte (lei)   _____
8. Capisce (lui)   _____
9. Lavoriamo   _____
10. Sentite   _____
11. Ascoltate   _____
12. Leggono   _____
13. Non ascoltate   _____
14. Andate   _____
15. Parto   _____
16. Arriva   _____
17. Piove   _____
18. So   _____
19. Conosci   _____
20. Puoi   _____
21. Non leggete   _____
22. Comprate   _____
23. Vendete   _____
24. Capite   _____

9. Practice

Rewrite the sentences, using the *present subjunctive* or *infinitive* of the verb in parentheses.

1. Io voglio che tu (andare) _____

2. Spero di (partire) _____

3. Dubitiamo che lui (arrivare) _____

4. Dubitiamo che lei (pensare) _____

5. Speri che io (visitare) _____

6. Speri di (andare) _____

7. Speriamo che lui (capire) _____

8. Speriamo di (comprare) _____

9. Pensate che io (vedere) _____

10. Penso che tu (potere) _____

11. Pensi che noi (volere) _____

12. Dubito che tu (leggere) _____

13. Speriamo di (finire) _____

14. Sperano che io (pagare) _____

15. Carlo vuole che io (ascoltare) _____

16. Penso che Mario (comprare) _____

17. Pensa che noi (vendere) _____

18. Pensa che tu (scrivere) _____

19. Penso che loro (guardare) _____

20. Dubito che tu (studiare) _____

21. È necessario che lui (partire) _____

22. È possibile che noi (rimanere) _____

23. Ho paura che voi (perdere) _____

24. Voglio che tu (rimanere) _____

Imperfect Subjunctive

10. Uses of the Imperfect Subjunctive

The imperfect subjunctive *(congiuntivo imperfetto),* like the present subjunctive, is used after certain verbs, impersonal expressions, and conjunctions. The main difference between these two tenses is the time of the action. If the action is in the present, the *present subjunctive* is used. If the action is related to the past, the *imperfect subjunctive* is used.

   If the verb of the main clause is expressed in the past tense or conditional, the *imperfect subjunctive* is used in the dependent *che* clause.

   Example: Paola pensava che *io arrivassi.*   Paola thought I would arrive.

11. Forms of the Imperfect Subjunctive

The *imperfect subjunctive* of all regular verbs and almost all irregular verbs is formed by adding the endings *ssi, ssi, sse, ssimo, ste, ssero* to the 1st person singular of the imperfect indicative after omitting the final **vo.**

Infinitive	Imperfect Indicative	Imperfect Subjunctive
Parlare	Parlavo	che io parlassi
Leggere	Leggevo	che io leggessi
Sentire	Sentivo	che io sentissi

The following chart shows the forms of the *imperfect subjunctive* of the regular *-are, -ere, -ire* verbs.

	Parlare	**Scrivere**	**Sentire**
che io	parla*ssi*	scrive*ssi*	senti*ssi*
che tu	parla*ssi*	scrive*ssi*	senti*ssi*
che lui	parla*sse*	scrive*sse*	senti*sse*
che lei	parla*sse*	scrive*sse*	senti*sse*
che noi	parla*ssimo*	scrive*ssimo*	senti*ssimo*
che voi	parla*ste*	scrive*ste*	senti*ste*
che loro	parla*ssero*	scrive*ssero*	senti*ssero*

The following verbs have *irregular* forms of the *imperfect subjunctive.*

stare	*stessi, stessi, stesse, stessimo, steste, stessero*
essere	*fossi, fossi, fosse, fossimo, foste, fossero*
dare	*dessi, dessi, desse, dessimo, deste, dessero*
dire	*dicessi, dicessi, dicesse, dicessimo, diceste, dicessero*
fare	*facessi, facessi, facesse, facessimo, faceste, facessero*

12. Practice

Write the *imperfect subjunctive* of the verbs.

1. **ascoltare**   che io_____   che tu_____   che lui, lei_____

   (to listen)   che noi_____   che voi_____   che loro_____

2. **conoscere**   che io_____   che tu_____   che lui, lei_____

   (to know)   che noi_____   che voi_____   che loro_____

3. **venire**   che io_____   che tu_____   che lui, lei_____

   (to come)   che noi_____   che voi_____   che loro_____

13. Practice

Write the verbs in the *imperfect subjunctive* in the person indicated.

Che io:

parlare   leggere   pulire

_____   _____   _____

Che tu:

comprare   vedere   finire

_____   _____   _____

Che lui:

andare   potere   sentire

_____   _____   _____

Che lei:

arrivare   correre   partire

_____   _____   _____

Che noi:

dimenticare   bere   dormire

_____   _____   _____

Che voi:

perdonare   scrivere   venire

_____   _____   _____

Che loro:

studiare   temere   capire

_____   _____   _____

14. Practice

Write the verbs in the *imperfect subjunctive* in the person indicated.

Pensavo che tu:

fare   vincere   capire

_____   _____   _____

Pensavo che lui:

lavorare   perdere   finire

_____   _____   _____

Pensavo che lei:

studiare   correggere   sentire

_____   _____   _____

Pensavo che noi:

cambiare   sapere   dormire

_____   _____   _____

Pensavo che voi:

sognare   accendere   costruire

_____   _____   _____

Pensavo che loro:

insegnare   spegnere   venire

_____   _____   _____

Speravo che tu:

parlare   vedere   finire

_____   _____   _____

Speravo che voi:

fare   leggere   pulire

_____   _____   _____

15. Practice

Rewrite in Italian, using the *imperfect subjunctive.* Sometimes an *infinitive* will be needed.

1. I wanted you (s.) to come _____

2. I hoped you (s.) would come _____

3. You thought you (s.) could study _____

4. You (s.) thought he would study _____

5. You (s.) thought we would come _____

6. I hoped you (pl.) would come _____

7. I believed he would write _____

8. I thought we would go _____

9. You (s.) hoped they would call _____

10. They thought I would remain _____

11. You all thought he would play _____

12. I thought you (s.) would clean _____

13. I did not know you (s.) would go _____

14. You (s.) wanted me to cook _____

15. She would like you (s.) to read _____

16. It would be necessary for you (s.) to leave _____

17. My father wanted me to work _____

18. It was difficult for you (s.) to go _____

19. I did not know you (s.) were so tall _____

20. She wanted me to ask the doctor _____

21. I wished to sleep all day long _____

22. I wished she slept all day long _____

23. He wanted us to go _____

24. I hoped they invited me _____

16. Practice

Change the verbs in parentheses to the *present subjunctive* or to the *imperfect subjunctive* as needed.

1. Spero che tu (parlare) _____
2. Speravo che tu (parlare) _____
3. Dubito che noi (venire) _____
4. Dubitavo che noi (venire) _____
5. Pensiamo che lui (essere) _____
6. Pensavamo che lui (essere) _____
7. È probabile che io (studiare) _____
8. Era probabile che lui (studiare) _____
9. È necessario che voi (studiare) _____
10. Era necessario che voi (studiare) _____
11. Credo di (venire) _____
12. Credevo di (venire) _____
13. Dubitiamo che lui (imparare) _____
14. Dubitavamo che lui (imparare) _____
15. Credo che tu (sognare) _____
16. Credeva che tu (sognare) _____
17. È possibile che loro (fare) _____
18. Era possibile che loro (fare) _____
19. Penso che voi (ricordare) _____
21. Spera che lui (arrivare) _____
22. Speravo che lui (arrivare) _____
23. Voglio che tu (scrivere) _____
24. Volevo che tu (scrivere) _____

Chapter 8

Past Subjunctive

1. Use of the Past Subjunctive

The past subjunctive *(congiuntivo passato)* is used in a dependent *che* clause to express the speaker's feelings toward a recent past action when the verb in the main clause is in the present indicative. The present of *avere* or *essere* and the *past participle* of the verb are used.

Example: Credo che *abbiano vinto* la partita.   I think that they won the game.

Note that the action in the *che* clause is in the past in relation to the action in the main clause, which is in the present tense.

2. Forms of the Past Subjunctive

The following chart shows the conjugations of *trovare, vedere, partire* in the past subjunctive.

	Trovare (To find)	**Credere** (To believe)	**Sentire** (To hear)
che io	abbia trovato	abbia creduto	abbia sentito
che tu	abbia trovato	abbia creduto	abbia sentito
che lui	abbia trovato	abbia creduto	abbia sentito
che lei	abbia trovato	abbia creduto	abbia sentito
che noi	abbiamo trovato	abbiamo creduto	abbiamo sentito
che voi	abbiate trovato	abbiate creduto	abbiate sentito
che loro	abbiano trovato	abbiano creduto	abbiano sentito

Conjugation of the past subjunctive using *essere*

	Partire (To leave, to depart)
che io	sia partito/a
che tu	sia partito/a
che lui	sia partito
che lei	sia partita
che noi	siamo partiti/e
che voi	siate partiti/e
che loro	siano partiti/e

3. Practice

Write the *past subjunctive* of the verbs in the person indicated.

Che io:
arrivare ___ vedere ___ finire ___

___

Che tu:
parlare ___ leggere ___ capire ___

___

Che lui:
ascoltare ___ scrivere ___ sentire ___

___

Che lei:
piantare ___ scendere ___ salire ___

___

Che noi:
studiare ___ vendere ___ sostituire ___

___

Che voi:
cancellare ___ bere ___ venire ___

___

Che loro:
guardare ___ mantenere ___ partire ___

___

Che io:
non sperare ___ non aspettare ___ non ridere ___

___

4. Practice

Complete the sentences with the *past subjunctive.*

1. È bene che Paolo (venire) _____

2. Speriamo che lui (parlare) _____

3. Loro sono contenti che noi (studiare) _____

4. Mi dispiace che tu (perdere) _____

5. Sono contento che noi (andare) _____

6. È giusto che lui (pagare) _____

7. È possibile che la polizia (arrestare) _____

8. Ci dispiace che tu non (trovare) _____

9. Ci dispiace che voi non (mangiare) _____

10. È bene che Maria (partire) _____

11. Sono sorpreso che lui (telefonare) _____

12. È sorpreso che voi (telefonare) _____

13. È possibile che lei non (studiare) _____

14. Spero che loro (venire) _____

15. Spero che voi (nuotare) _____

16. È giusto che io (ritornare) _____

17. È impossibile che lui (finire) _____

18. Siamo contenti che lui (capire) _____

19. Non credo che tu (trovare) _____

20. È possibile che Carlo (partire) _____

21. È necessario che tu (scrivere) _____

22. Siamo contenti che loro (studiare) _____

23. Sono sorpreso che tu (studiare) _____

24. Ci dispiace che lui non (telefonare) _____

5. Practice

Write the verbs in three forms of the *subjunctive: present, imperfect, past.*

Present	Imperfect	Past
1. Che io parlare		
2. Che tu sentire		
3. Che lui capire		
4. Che lei venire		
5. Che noi offrire		
6. Che voi prendere		
7. Che loro vedere		
8. Che io non pensare		
9. Che tu non leggere		
10. Che lui non pulire		
11. Che noi non stare		

Pluperfect Subjunctive

6. Use of the Pluperfect Subjunctive

The pluperfect subjunctive *(congiuntivo trapassato)* is used when the action of the verb in the dependent clause happened before the action of the verb in the main clause, which is in the past.

It is formed by the imperfect subjunctive of *essere* and *avere* plus the *past participle* of the verb.

Example:

Pres. Ind.	Perfect Subj.	Imp. Ind.	Pluperfect Subj.

Credo che Mario sia venuto.
I think that Mario came.

Credevo che Mario fosse venuto.
I thought that Mario had come.

7. Forms of the Pluperfect Subjunctive

The following chart shows the conjugations of the *pluperfect subjunctive* with *essere* and *avere.*

	Partire	Capire
che io	*fossi partito/a*	*avessi capito*
che tu	*fossi partito/a*	*avessi capito*
che lui/lei	*fosse partito/a*	*avesse capito*
che noi	*fossimo partiti/e*	*avessimo capito*
che voi	*foste partiti/e*	*aveste capito*
che loro	*fossero partiti/e*	*avessero capito*

8. Practice

Rewrite in English.

1. Che io fossi arrivato _____

2. Che tu avessi pensato _____

3. Che noi fossimo partiti _____

4. Che voi aveste parlato _____

5. Che loro fossero venuti _____

9. Practice

Rewrite the sentences, using the *imperfect subjunctive* in the main clause and the *pluperfect subjunctive* in the *che* clause.

1. Sembra che sappia tutto (lui) _____

2. È possibile che arrivi (lei) _____

3. Speriamo che entri (lei) _____

4. Penso che lui arrivi _____

5. Dubito che sappia (tu) _____

6. Sembra che capisca (lui) _____

7. È meglio che tu vada _____

8. È meglio che loro partano _____

9. Sembra che io sappia _____

10. Preferisco che voi andiate _____

11. Preferiamo che tu studi _____

12. Sono sicuro che Carlo arrivi _____

13. Preferisce che impariamo _____

14. Sono contento che tu venga _____

15. Siamo sicuri che partano _____

16. È probabile che tu arrivi _____

17. Penso che tu venga _____

18. Dubito che lui trovi lavoro _____

19. Credo che lei cerchi lavoro _____

20. È necessario che io legga _____

21. È bene che loro comprino _____

22. È necessario che vendano _____

23. Spero che Carlo venda _____

Se Clauses and the Subjunctive

10. Contrary-to-Fact

To express a *contrary-to-fact* statement in the present or the future, the *imperfect subjunctive* is used in the *se clause.* The conditional is normally used in the main clause to express a conclusion to the action.

    Example: *Se potessi,* verrei.   If I could, I would come.

To express a contrary-to-fact statement in the past, the pluperfect subjunctive is used in the *se clause* and the past conditional is used in the main clause.

    Example: *Se avessi saputo, sarei venuto.*   If I had known, I would have come.

11. Wishes

Se + the *imperfect subjunctive* is used in exclamations to express wishes that may never materialize.

    Examples: *Se avessi* tanti soldi!   If only I had a lot of money!
                      Se potessi parlare!   If only I could talk!

12. Practice

Use the verbs in parentheses in the correct tense of the subjunctive.

1.   Capirei se tu (spiegare) _____

2.   Studieresti se (potere) _____

3.   Compreremmo se (avere) i soldi _____

4.   Scriverebbe se (sapere) _____

5.   Verrebbe se (guidare) _____

6.   Avrebbe capito se tu (spiegare) _____

7.   Avrebbe studiato se (potere) _____

8.   Avremmo comprato se (avere) soldi _____

9.   Avrebbe scritto se (sapere) _____

10. Sarebbe venuto se (guidare) _____

11. Avresti comprato se lui (vendere) _____

12. Sarei andato se (sapere) _____

13. Avresti parlato se tu (potere) _____

14. Avreste capito se voi (studiare) _____

Reflexive Verbs

13. The Nature of Reflexive Verbs

A reflexive verb *(verbo riflessivo)* is one in which the object of the verb is the same person or thing as the subject. They are more common in Italian than in English.

Examples:	*Mi pettino.*	I comb my hair.
	Mi sveglio presto.	I wake up early.
	Carlo *si diverte.*	Carlo enjoys himself.

Some Italian verbs have both reflexive and nonreflexive forms.

Examples:	Noi *laviamo* tutti i giorni.	We wash every day.
	Noi *ci laviamo* tutti i giorni.	We wash ourselves every day.

Plural reflexive verbs used with the reflexive pronouns *ci, vi,* and *si* express a reciprocal meaning.

Example:	*Ci vediamo* ogni lunedì.	We see each other every Monday.
	Si scrivono spesso.	They write each other often.

Note: In Italian, the *reflexive* is often used where English uses an impersonal construction or the passive.

Examples:	Qui *si parla* italiano.	Here one speaks Italian.
	Come *si va* alla stazione?	How do you go to the station?
	Come *si fa* la pizza?	How do you make pizza?

14. Forms of Reflexive Verbs

In the present tense, the reflexive pronoun comes before the verb, but in the infinitive it is attached to the end, with the final *e* of the infinitive dropped.

Examples:	*Mi lavo* subito.	I wash myself right away.
	Vado a *lavarmi* subito.	I'm going to wash myself right away.

In the passato prossimo, reflexive verbs always use the auxiliary *essere* and a past participle that agrees with the subject.

Examples:	Giovanni *si è* addormentato.	Giovanni fell asleep.
	Carla *si è* addormentata.	Carla fell asleep.

Following is the conjugation of the present tense of *alzarsi*. The other tenses follow the same patterns of the regular verbs with the exception of the pronoun, which has to be placed in front of the verb.

Alzarsi			To get up
io	mi	alzo	I get up
tu	ti	alzi	you get up
lui	si	alza	he gets up
lei	si	alza	she gets up
noi	ci	alziamo	we get up
voi	vi	alzate	you get up
loro	si	alzano	they get up

15. List of Common Reflexive Verbs

Here is a list of some common reflexive verbs in Italian. They are not necessarily reflexive in English.

addormentarsi	to fall asleep
aiutarsi	to help one another
alzarsi	to get up
amarsi	to love each other
chiamarsi	to be called
divertirsi	to enjoy oneself, to have a good time
incontrarsi	to meet each other
innamorarsi	to fall in love
lavarsi	to wash oneself
mettersi	to put on (clothing)
mettersi a	to start, to begin
odiarsi	to hate one another
parlarsi	to speak to each other
prepararsi	to get ready
salutarsi	to greet one another
scriversi	to write each other
sentirsi	to feel
svegliarsi	to wake up
vedersi	to see each other
vestirsi	to get dressed

16. Practice

Write the verbs in the present indicative in the person indicated.

Io:

alzarsi   mettersi   sentirsi

_____   _____   _____

Tu:

addormentarsi   pettinarsi   domandarsi

_____   _____   _____

Lui:

lavarsi   pettinarsi   vestirsi

_____   _____   _____

Lei:

divertirsi   sposarsi   prepararsi

_____   _____   _____

Noi:

vestirsi   svegliarsi   aiutarsi

_____   _____   _____

Voi:

parlarsi   salutarsi   incontrarsi

_____   _____   _____

Loro:

divertirsi   sposarsi   prepararsi

_____   _____   _____

17. Practice

Rewrite in English.

1. Si sveglia (lui) _____

2. Lei si veste _____

3. Loro si preparano _____

4. Ci prepariamo _____

5. Vi salutate _____

6. Si parlano _____

7. Vi odiate _____

8. Si amano _____

9. Si mette a parlare _____

10. Si scrivono _____

11. Mi alzo _____

12. Ti lavi _____

13. Si lava (lui) _____

14. Carlo si veste _____

15. Ci incontriamo _____

16. Mi vesto _____

17. Si addormenta _____

18. Vi parlate _____

19. Si aiutano _____

20. Mi addormento _____

21. Si pettina (lui) _____

22. Si specchiano _____

23. Vi preparate _____

24. Si inginocchiano _____

18. Practice

Rewrite in Italian.

1. We wake up _____

2. I enjoy myself _____

3. They get up _____

4. They wake up _____

5. They greet each other _____

6. They get ready _____

7. He washes himself _____

8. She combs her hair _____

9. They meet each other _____

10. They enjoy themselves _____

11. She enjoys herself _____

12. He gets ready _____

13. You (pl.) get dressed _____

14. I get dressed _____

15. We help each other _____

16. We get up _____

17. We wake up _____

18. We love each other _____

19. We woke up _____

20. He got up _____

21. You (s.) washed yourself _____

22. She combed her hair _____

23. They hated each other _____

24. He enjoyed himself _____

Chapter 9

Progressive Tenses

1. Uses of the Progressive Tenses

In Italian, often the present and the imperfect tenses are used to express continuing actions, while in English the progressive tenses are generally used.

Examples:	*Mangiano.*	*They are eating.*
	Scrivo una lettera di affari.	*I am writing* a business letter.
	Parlavano.	*They were talking.*

In Italian, the progressive tense is used when one wants to emphasize that the action is going on at the time of speaking.

There are two progressive tenses: *present progressive* and *past progressive.*

Present Progressive:	Dove *stai andando?*	Where are you going?
Past Progressive:	Dove *stavi andando?*	Where were you going?

2. Forms of the Progressive

The progressive tenses are formed with the verb *stare* + the *gerund.* The gerund is formed by adding *-ando, -endo, -endo* forms to the infinitive stem of *-are, -ere,* and *-ire* verbs respectively.

Examples:	parlare	*parlando*
	tenere	*tenendo*
	sentire	*sentendo*

The present of *stare* is used for the *present progressive,* and the imperfect of *stare* is used for the *past progressive.*

Following are the complete conjugations of the *present progressive* and the *past progressive*.

Present Progressive			Past Progressive		
io	sto	parlando *(I am speaking)*	io	stavo	parlando *(I was speaking)*
tu	stai	parlando	tu	stavi	parlando
lui	sta	parlando	lui	stava	parlando
lei	sta	parlando	lei	stava	parlando
noi	stiamo	parlando	noi	stavamo	parlando
voi	state	parlando	voi	stavate	parlando
loro	stanno	parlando	loro	stavano	parlando

Note: Reflexive pronouns may precede or follow *stare.*

> **Example:** Lei *si sta pettinando.*   She is combing her hair.
>
> or
>
> Lei *sta pettinandosi.*   She is combing her hair.

3. Practice

Change the present tense into the *present progressive* and the imperfect to the *past progressive.*

A.

1. Io parlo _____

2. Tu ascolti _____

3. Noi parliamo_____

4. Lui guida _____

5. Lei sente _____

6. Noi studiamo _____

7. Voi partite_____

8. Tu leggi _____

9. Lei parla _____

10. Io gioco_____

11. Tu parti _____

12. Loro tornano_____

B.

1. Tu andavi _____

2. Tu ascoltavi _____

3. Voi parlavate _____

4. Io bevevo _____

5. Voi vedevate_____

6. Noi giocavamo _____

7. Voi scrivevate_____

8. Lui leggeva _____

9. Tu prendevi _____

10. Io bevevo _____

11. Tu partivi _____

12. Io tornavo _____

Modal Verbs

4. Common Modal Verbs

A *modal verb* is a special verb usually followed by an infinitive. The common modal verbs are:

dovere (must, to have to, should)	expresses duty
potere (to be able to, can)	expresses ability
volere (to want)	expresses wants

Devo studiare.	I must (have to) study.
Possono rimanere.	They can stay.
Vogliamo pagare.	We want to pay.

Note: All *modal verbs* are sometimes used without the infinitive, mainly in responses.

> **Examples:** *Puoi leggere* un po'? Can you read a little?
> No, non *posso.* No, I can't.

The modal verbs are conjugated with *avere* in the compound tenses when the infinitive following the modal verb is transitive, with *essere* if the infinitive is intransitive.

> **Examples:** Maria *ha dovuto* pagare. Mary had to pay.
> Maria *è dovuta andare* a pagare. Mary had to go to pay.

5. Forms of the Modal Verbs

	Dovere	**Volere**	**Potere**
Present:	devo	voglio	posso
	devi	vuoi	puoi
	deve	vuole	può
	dobbiamo	vogliamo	possiamo
	dovete	volete	potete
	devono	vogliono	possono
Future:	dovrò	vorrò	potrò
	dovrai	vorrai	potrai
	dovrà	vorrà	potrà
	dovremo	vorremo	potremo
	dovrete	vorrete	potrete
	dovranno	vorranno	potranno
Imperf.:	dovevo	volevo	potevo
	dovevi	volevi	potevi
	etc.	etc.	etc.

	Dovere	**Volere**	**Potere**
Passato Prossimo:	ho (sono) dovuto hai (sei) dovuto etc.	ho (sono) voluto hai (sei) voluto etc.	ho (sono) potuto hai (sei) potuto etc.
Present Condit.:	dovrei dovresti dovrebbe dovremmo dovreste dovrebbero	vorrei vorresti vorrebbe vorremmo vorreste vorrebbero	potrei potresti potrebbe potremmo potreste potrebbero
Past Condit.:	avrei (sarei) dovuto avresti (saresti) dovuto etc.	avrei (sarei) voluto avresti (saresti) voluto etc.	avrei (sarei) potuto avresti (saresti) potuto etc.
Present Subjunct.:	che io, tu, lui debba che noi dobbiamo che voi dobbiate che loro debbano	che io, tu, lui voglia che noi vogliamo che voi vogliate che loro vogliano	che io, tu, lui possa che noi possiamo che voi possiate che loro possano
Imperfect Subjunct.:	dovessi dovessi dovesse dovessimo doveste dovessero	volessi volessi volesse volessimo voleste volessero	potessi potessi potesse potessimo poteste potessero
Past Subjunct.:	avessi (fossi) dovuto avessi (fossi) dovuto avesse (fosse) dovuto etc.	avessi (fossi) voluto avessi (fossi) voluto avesse (fosse) voluto etc.	avessi (fossi) potuto avessi (fossi) potuto avesse (fosse) potuto etc.

Note: When **dovere, volere, potere** are conjugated with the verb *essere,* the past participle of the verb agrees in gender and number with the subject.

6. Practice

Rewrite in English.

Voglio andare

_____

Devo studiare

_____

Posso portare

_____

Volevamo partire

_____

Dovevamo arrivare

_____

Potevamo sentire

_____

Vorrà portare

_____

Dovrà correre

_____

Potrà comprare

_____

Hanno voluto ascoltare

_____

Hanno dovuto fare

_____

Hanno potuto dire

_____

Sono voluti venire

_____

Sono dovuti andare

_____

Sono potuti partire

_____

7. Practice

Rewrite in Italian.

I want to think

_____

I must go

_____

I can sing

_____

You (s.) wanted to write

_____

You (s.) had to see

_____

You (s.) could sell (past)

_____

We would like to come

_____

We should buy

_____

We could read (possibility)

_____

They have wanted to play

_____

They have had to close

_____

They could have cleaned

_____

The Passive Voice

In the *active voice* studied so far, the subject performs the action. In the *passive voice,* the subject receives the action.

Examples:

Active Voice	*Passive Voice*
Maria *cucina* la cena.	La cena *è cucinata* da Maria.
Mary *cooks* dinner.	Dinner *is cooked* by Mary.
Maria *ha cucinato* la cena	La cena *è stata cucinata* da Maria.
Mary *cooked* dinner.	The dinner *was cooked* by Mary.

The *passive* in Italian is formed as in English, with the verb *essere* and the *past participle* of the verb needed. The past participle agrees with the subject in gender and number. The reflexive form is used instead of the *passive* in Italian when the person doing the action is not mentioned.

Examples:

La lettera *fu spedita*	The letter was mailed
ieri da mio padre.	yesterday by my father.
Si sono spedite le lettere ieri.	The letters were mailed yesterday.

8. Practice

Rewrite in English.

1. Quando è stato pagato il conto? _____

2. Da chi è stata scritta la Divina Commedia? _____

3. L'America è stata scoperta nel 1492. _____

4. Il ragazzo è stato svegliato. _____

5. La casa è finita. _____

9. Practice

Rewrite in Italian.

1. English is studied by many. _____

2. The game was played in the rain. _____

3. When was the dog found? _____

4. The house is cleaned by Paul. _____

5. The car was sold quickly. _____

Verbs That Follow Common Patterns

Many verbs in Italian are conjugated like other irregular verbs. By knowing the common verbs, you can conjugate many other verbs. Study these examples.

Dire

benedire	to bless
contraddire	to contradict
disdire	to retract
maledire	to curse
interdire	to forbid
predire	to predict

Fare

assuefarsi	to get accustomed
contraffare	to imitate
disfare	to undo
rifare	to redo
soddisfare	to satisfy
stupefare	to amaze

Porre

deporre	to put down
opporre	to oppose
proporre	to propose
supporre	to suppose

Prendere

contendere	to compete, to quarrel
distendere	to relax
estendere	to extend
fraintendere	to misunderstand
pretendere	to claim

Vedere

avvedersi	to become aware
intravedere	to glimpse
prevedere	to foresee
rivedere	to see again, to review

Venire

addivenire	to come to an agreement
divenire	to become
intervenire	to intervene
pervenire	to reach
prevenire	to anticipate

Cogliere

distogliere	to dissuade
raccogliere	to gather
togliere	to remove

Tenere

attenersi	to keep, to stick to
contenere	to contain
ottenere	to obtain

10. Practice

Write the verbs in the tense and person indicated.

Present

1. io (disdire) _____
2. tu (rifare) _____
3. voi (fraintendere) _____
4. loro (intervenire) _____
5. io (togliere)_____

6. lei (rifare) _____
7. loro (supporre) _____
8. lui (ottenere) _____
9. loro (interdire) _____
10. noi (rivedere) _____

Future

1. io (rifare) _____
2. loro (contendere) _____
3. lui (supporre) _____
4. noi (prevedere) _____
5. voi (rifare) _____

6. noi (opporre) _____
7. loro (ottenere)_____
8. io (predire) _____
9. lei (contraddire) _____
10. loro (intervenire) _____

Passato Remoto

1. loro (addivenire)_____
2. lui (prevedere) _____
3. loro (soddisfare)_____
4. noi (predire) _____
5. io (togliere)_____

6. voi (fraintendere) _____
7. lei (proporre) _____
8. loro (contraddire) _____
9. tu (prevenire) _____
10. loro (contraffare) _____

Passato Prossimo

1. io (stupefare) _____
2. tu (opporre) _____
3. noi (disdire) _____

4. loro (prevedere) _____
5. lei (ottenere) _____
6. tu (pretendere) _____

11. Practice

Rewrite in Italian. Use the *present, future,* or *passato remoto.*

1. They predicted _____

2. We'll relax _____

3. He becomes _____

4. We'll reach _____

5. She'll forbid _____

6. They supposed _____

7. They imitate _____

8. We anticipate _____

9. He'll foresee _____

10. You (s.) oppose _____

11. They'll satisfy _____

12. You (pl.) misunderstand _____

13. She gathered _____

14. You (s.) contradict _____

15. We competed _____

16. I'll remove _____

17. They'll amaze _____

18. He became aware _____

19. I redo _____

20. You relaxed _____

21. We suppose _____

22. I proposed _____

23. We dissuade _____

24. She gathers _____

25. I'll retract _____

26. We'll imitate _____

27. You (s.) oppose _____

28. You (pl.) became _____

29. We removed _____

30. She intervened _____

Chapter 10

General Review of Verbs

1. Present

Write the verbs in the *present indicative* in the person indicated.

Io:

parlare   vedere   sentire   capire

_____ _____ _____ _____

Tu:

camminare   scrivere   partire   finire

_____ _____ _____ _____

Lui:

lavorare   leggere   venire   pulire

_____ _____ _____ _____

Lei:

cucinare   temere   dire   uscire

_____ _____ _____ _____

Noi:

insegnare   volere   scoprire   offrire

_____ _____ _____ _____

Voi:

arrivare   vincere   avvenire   riuscire

_____ _____ _____ _____

Loro:

cambiare   perdere   morire   salire

_____ _____ _____ _____

2. Imperfect

Write the verbs in the *imperfect* in the person indicated.

io cominciare	tu parlare	lui arrivare	lei mangiare
_____	_____	_____	_____
lui perdere	lei vincere	noi dire	loro dare
_____	_____	_____	_____
noi venire	tu capire	lei finire	io salire
_____	_____	_____	_____
io parlare	tu diventare	lei comprare	noi passare
_____	_____	_____	_____
tu leggere	noi essere	voi scrivere	loro dovere
_____	_____	_____	_____
noi finire	voi dire	loro capire	tu finire
_____	_____	_____	_____
io chiudere	tu arrivare	lui partire	lei uscire
_____	_____	_____	_____
noi cambiare	voi scrivere	loro entrare	tu fuggire
_____	_____	_____	_____
io avere	tu dovere	noi andare	lui essere
_____	_____	_____	_____
noi potere	tu fare	lei uscire	loro volere
_____	_____	_____	_____
loro venire	lei dire	loro uscire	lei finire
_____	_____	_____	_____
io andare	loro capire	voi finire	tu partire
_____	_____	_____	_____

3. Future

A. Rewrite in English.

1. Mangerò _____

2. Sentirai _____

3. Salirà (lui) _____

4. Compreremo _____

5. Faremo _____

6. Studierò _____

7. Sentirò _____

8. Ascolterà _____

9. Partirete _____

10. Capirete _____

11. Farò _____

12. Vorrai _____

13. Dovrete _____

14. Vi alzerete _____

15. Guiderò _____

16. Voleremo _____

17. Fermerai _____

18. Saprò _____

19. Conoscerò _____

20. Arriveremo _____

21. Starò _____

22. Saremo _____

23. Leggerete _____

B. Rewrite in Italian.

1. I will go _____

2. You will sleep _____

3. He will eat _____

4. I will clean _____

5. She will walk _____

6. You (pl.) will call _____

7. I will listen _____

8. You (s.) will change _____

9. We will stay _____

10. They will enter _____

11. I will laugh _____

12. We will be able _____

13. I will see _____

14. You (pl.) will go _____

15. They will write _____

16. He will answer _____

17. I will have to _____

18. I will forget _____

19. She will clean _____

20. They will stay _____

21. I will do _____

22. She will close _____

23. They will drink _____

4. Passato Remoto and Passato Prossimo

Change the infinitive first into the *passato remoto,* then into the *passato prossimo.*

	Passato Remoto	Passato Prossimo
Io: andare	_____	_____
Tu: fare	_____	_____
Lui: venire	_____	_____
Lei: capire	_____	_____
Noi: vedere	_____	_____
Voi: pensare	_____	_____
Loro: sentire	_____	_____
Io: stare	_____	_____
Tu: chiedere	_____	_____
Lui: mandare	_____	_____
Lei: pensare	_____	_____

5. Trapassato Prossimo

A. Rewrite in English.

B. Rewrite in Italian, using the *trapassato prossimo.*

1. Avevo mangiato _____
2. Avevamo capito _____
3. Avevano dormito _____
4. Erano partiti _____
5. Ero andato_____
6. Eravamo stati _____
7. Avevamo parlato _____
8. Avevi studiato_____
9. Avevo capito_____
10. Avevo chiuso _____
11. Avevi sentito _____
12. Avevamo portato _____
13. Aveva perso (lui) _____
14. Avevate vinto _____
15. Avevo telefonato _____
16. Aveva finito (lei) _____
17. Ero stato _____
18. Erano saliti _____
19. Era scesa (lei)_____
20. Eravate partiti_____
21. Eravamo dispiaciute_____
22. Erano morti_____
23. Ero entrata _____

1. I had slept_____
2. He had entered _____
3. She had spoken _____
4. We had understood _____
5. You (pl.) had made _____
6. He had done _____
7. She had written _____
8. You (s.) had been _____
9. She had seen _____
10. We had come _____
11. They had returned _____
12. We had gone _____
13. I had eaten _____
14. You (s.) had written_____
15. They had cleaned_____
16. We had read_____
17. She had put _____
18. We had told _____
19. I had known _____
20. He had seen _____
21. I had wanted _____
22. You (pl.) had said _____
23. She was born _____

6. Present Conditional

Rewrite in Italian, using the *present conditional.*

1. I would like _____

2. I would read _____

3. You (pl.) would speak _____

4. She would listen _____

5. I would clean _____

6. They would write _____

7. We would think _____

8. I would answer _____

9. You (s.) would read _____

10. He would eat _____

11. She would sell _____

12. We would study _____

13. I would ski _____

14. They would travel _____

15. You (pl.) would drink _____

16. I would study _____

17. I should _____

18. I could _____

19. You (s.) would want _____

20. We would think _____

21. They would close _____

22. We would open _____

23. She would understand _____

7. Past Conditional

Rewrite in Italian, using the *past conditional.*

1. I would have liked
    _____

2. I would have been
    _____

3. She would have spoken
    _____

4. I would have listened
    _____

5. You (pl.) would have cleaned
    _____

6. They would have written
    _____

7. They would have thought
    _____

8. He would have read
    _____

9. We would have eaten
    _____

10. They would have arrived
    _____

11. I would have been
    _____

12. We would have stayed
    _____

13. You (s.) would have drunk
    _____

14. He would have studied
    _____

15. She would have gone
    _____

16. You (pl.) would have wanted
    _____

17. I would have closed
    _____

18. He would have opened
    _____

19. She would have thought
    _____

20. We would have understood
    _____

21. They would have traveled
    _____

22. You (s.) would have sung
    _____

23. They would have looked
    _____

24. We would have come
    _____

8. Present Subjunctive and Imperfect Subjunctive

Change the infinitive to the *present* and *imperfect subjunctive* in the person indicated.

		Present Subjunctive	Imperfect Subjunctive
1.	Che io mangiare	_____	_____
2.	Che tu vedere	_____	_____
3.	Che lui parlare	_____	_____
4.	Che lei sentire	_____	_____
5.	Che noi chiudere	_____	_____
6.	Che voi capire	_____	_____
7.	Che loro venire	_____	_____
8.	Che noi rispondere	_____	_____
9.	Che tu scrivere	_____	_____
10.	Che io imparare	_____	_____
11.	Che lui finire	_____	_____
12.	Che noi mangiare	_____	_____
13.	Che voi bere	_____	_____
14.	Che loro sapere	_____	_____
15.	Che tu telefonare	_____	_____
16.	Che lei prendere	_____	_____
17.	Che voi stare	_____	_____
18.	Che io stare	_____	_____
19.	Che voi dovere	_____	_____
20.	Che loro capire	_____	_____
21.	Che lei leggere	_____	_____
22.	Che tu mandare	_____	_____
23.	Che lui vendere	_____	_____

9. Past Subjunctive and Pluperfect Subjunctive

Change the following verbs to the *past subjunctive* and *pluperfect subjunctive*.

		Past Subjunctive	Pluperfect Subjunctive
1.	Che io venire	_____	_____
2.	Che lui parlare	_____	_____
3.	Che noi ascoltare	_____	_____
4.	Che lei fare	_____	_____
5.	Che voi finire	_____	_____
6.	Che voi andare	_____	_____
7.	Che loro chiudere	_____	_____
8.	Che tu aprire	_____	_____
9.	Che io potere	_____	_____
10.	Che lei dire	_____	_____
11.	Che noi finire	_____	_____
12.	Che tu capire	_____	_____
13.	Che io rispondere	_____	_____
14.	Che lei vedere	_____	_____
15.	Che voi parlare	_____	_____
16.	Che io vivere	_____	_____
17.	Che lei prendere	_____	_____
18.	Che loro viaggiare	_____	_____
19.	Che io ordinare	_____	_____
20.	Che voi insegnare	_____	_____
21.	Che tu bere	_____	_____
22.	Che lei aspettare	_____	_____
23.	Che tu ricevere	_____	_____

10. Present, Future, Imperfect, Passato Remoto

Change the following verbs to the tense and person indicated.

	Present	Future	Imperfect	Passato Remoto
Io fare	_____	_____	_____	_____
Tu andare	_____	_____	_____	_____
Lui mangiare	_____	_____	_____	_____
Lei parlare	_____	_____	_____	_____
Noi leggere	_____	_____	_____	_____
Voi bere	_____	_____	_____	_____
Loro vedere	_____	_____	_____	_____
Io sentire	_____	_____	_____	_____
Lui dare	_____	_____	_____	_____
Voi stare	_____	_____	_____	_____
Lei capire	_____	_____	_____	_____
Loro finire	_____	_____	_____	_____
Io rispondere	_____	_____	_____	_____
Lui pulire	_____	_____	_____	_____
Noi arrivare	_____	_____	_____	_____
Voi salire	_____	_____	_____	_____
Tu soffrire	_____	_____	_____	_____
Lei offire	_____	_____	_____	_____
Io imparare	_____	_____	_____	_____
Lui vedere	_____	_____	_____	_____
Lei cadere	_____	_____	_____	_____
Lui morire	_____	_____	_____	_____

11. Passato Prossimo and Trapassato Prossimo

Change the infinitive into the *passato prossimo* and *trapassato prossimo*.

		Passato Prossimo	Trapassato Prossimo
1.	Io capire	_____	_____
2.	Tu vedere	_____	_____
3.	Lei finire	_____	_____
4.	Lui leggere	_____	_____
5.	Noi ritornare	_____	_____
6.	Voi imparare	_____	_____
7.	Loro cenare	_____	_____
8.	Io pranzare	_____	_____
9.	Lei vendere	_____	_____
10.	Lui accendere	_____	_____
11.	Voi accettare	_____	_____
12.	Loro spegnere	_____	_____
13.	Io lavare	_____	_____
14.	Noi uscire	_____	_____
15.	Tu viaggiare	_____	_____
16.	Lui partire	_____	_____
17.	Lei guarire	_____	_____
18.	Voi arrivare	_____	_____
19.	Tu ascoltare	_____	_____
20.	Loro saltare	_____	_____
21.	Lui esaminare	_____	_____
22.	Noi dividere	_____	_____
23.	Lei stirare	_____	_____

12. Present Conditional and Past Conditional

Change the infinitive into *present conditional* and *past conditional*.

		Present Conditional	Past Conditional
1.	Io parlare	_____	_____
2.	Tu arrivare	_____	_____
3.	Lui cantare	_____	_____
4.	Lei lavare	_____	_____
5.	Lui lavorare	_____	_____
6.	Noi stare	_____	_____
7.	Voi andare	_____	_____
8.	Loro viaggiare	_____	_____
9.	Io vedere	_____	_____
10.	Tu potere	_____	_____
11.	Lui leggere	_____	_____
12.	Lei scrivere	_____	_____
13.	Noi correre	_____	_____
14.	Voi rispondere	_____	_____
15.	Loro cadere	_____	_____
16.	Io capire	_____	_____
17.	Tu finire	_____	_____
18.	Lui venire	_____	_____
19.	Noi sentire	_____	_____
20.	Voi offrire	_____	_____
21.	Loro pulire	_____	_____

13. Subjunctive Forms

Change the infinitive into the *four* different *tenses* of the *subjunctive* as indicated.

	Present	Imperfect	Past	Pluperfect
Io andare				
Tu ritornare				
Lui dare				
Lei fare				
Noi stare				
Voi bere				
Loro vedere				
Noi fermare				
Lui sentire				
Lei dividere				
Lui pagare				
Tu vendere				
Io dormire				
Loro contare				
Voi dire				
Lei giocare				
Lui saltare				
Noi guardare				
Tu salire				
Voi leggere				
Loro tirare				
Noi pensare				

Chapter 11

Idiomatic Expressions with *Avere* and *Fare*

1. Idioms with the Verb *Avere*

Here are some common idioms with **avere.**

Note: The infinitive **avere** is frequently abbreviated to **aver** before a consonant. This usage is followed in the idioms presented below.

1.	**avere (aver) . . . anni**	to be . . . years old
2.	**aver bisogno (di)**	to need
3.	**aver caldo**	to feel (be) warm
4.	**aver fame**	to be hungry
5.	**aver freddo**	to be cold
6.	**aver fretta**	to be in a hurry
7.	**avere l'impressione (di)**	to have the impression
8.	**avere intenzione (di)**	to have the intention
9.	**aver mal (di)**	to have an ache
10.	**aver paura (di)**	to be afraid
11.	**aver ragione (di)**	to be right
12.	**aver sete**	to be thirsty
13.	**aver sonno**	to be sleepy
14.	**aver torto (di)**	to be wrong
15.	**aver vergogna (di)**	to be ashamed (of)
16.	**aver voglia (di)**	to feel like doing

2. Practice

Rewrite in Italian, using idiomatic expressions with *avere.*

1. I need shoes _____

2. I am warm _____

3. You are cold _____

4. We are in a hurry _____

5. They have a headache _____

6. I am afraid _____

7. She is thirsty _____

8. He was sleepy _____

9. They were right _____

10. I was wrong _____

11. We are ashamed _____

12. I feel like eating _____

13. You (pl.) were hungry _____

14. They were in a hurry _____

15. I would be thirsty _____

16. They would need shoes _____

17. She would be right _____

18. We would be wrong _____

19. I would be afraid _____

20. He would have the intention _____

21. I have had a headache _____

22. They have been afraid _____

23. We have been afraid _____

3. Idioms with the Verb *Fare*

The verb *fare* is used in many idiomatic expressions.

Note: The infinitive of *fare* is frequently abbreviated to *far* before a consonant.

1.	**fare alla romana**	to go Dutch
2.	**fare bella, brutta figura**	to make a good, bad impression
3.	**fare attenzione**	to pay attention
4.	**fare benzina**	to get gas
5.	**fa caldo, freddo**	it is warm, cold
6.	**fare carriera**	to be successful
7.	**fare colazione**	to have breakfast
8.	**fare colpo su qualcuno**	to impress someone
9.	**fare compere**	to go shopping
10.	**fare esercizio**	to exercise
11.	**fare fotografie**	to take pictures
12.	**fare il bagno**	to take a bath
13.	**fare la conoscenza di**	to make the acquaintance
14.	**fare una crociera**	to take a cruise
15.	**fare la doccia**	to take a shower
16.	**fare lo jogging**	to jog
17.	**fare il pieno**	to fill up with gas
18.	**fare la spesa**	to get groceries
19.	**fare male**	to hurt, to ache
20.	**fare parte di**	to be part of
21.	**fare una passeggiata**	to take a walk
22.	**fare presto**	to hurry up
23.	**fare progresso**	to progress

24.	**fare quattro chiacchiere**	to chat
25.	**fare il campeggio**	to go camping
26.	**fare un complimento**	to pay a compliment
27.	**fare un discorso**	to make a speech
28.	**fare la predica**	to preach
29.	**fare una domanda**	to ask a question
30.	**fare un giro**	to take a tour
31.	**fare uno spuntino**	to have a snack
32.	**fare un viaggio**	to take a trip
33.	**fare un regalo**	to give a gift
34.	**fare visita**	to pay a visit
35.	**farsi male**	to get hurt
36.	**fare un favore (a)**	to do a favor
37.	**fare un piacere (a)**	to do a favor
38.	**far vedere a qualcuno**	to show someone

Weather Expressions

Che tempo fa?	How is the weather?
Fa bel tempo (cattivo).	The weather is good (bad).
Fa caldo (freddo).	It is warm (cold).

4. Practice

Rewrite in Italian, using idiomatic expressions with *fare*.

1. We go Dutch _____

2. He pays attention _____

3. I have breakfast _____

4. We take a bath _____

5. They have taken a cruise _____

6. She goes shopping _____

7. You (s.) got hurt _____

8. I do a favor _____

9. They take a walk _____

10. I'll take pictures _____

11. She took a trip _____

12. You (pl.) ask a question _____

13. He has a snack _____

14. We hurry up _____

15. It is warm _____

16. We give a gift _____

17. I pay a visit _____

18. It was cold _____

19. He preaches _____

20. She'll make a speech _____

21. They chat _____

22. He made a bad impression _____

Verbs and Expressions Followed by Prepositions

5. Verbs and Expressions Followed by the Preposition *a*

A. Before a Noun or Pronoun

assistere a	to attend	**fare vedere a**	to show
assomigliare a	to resemble	**fare visita a**	to visit
credere a	to believe in	**fare un regalo a**	to give a present to
dare noia a	to bother	**giocare a**	to play a game
dar da mangiare a	to feed	**interessarsi a**	to be interested in
dare fastidio a	to bother	**partecipare a**	to participate in
dare retta a	to listen to	**pensare a**	to think about
dare torto a	to blame	**raccomandarsi a**	to ask favors of
dare la caccia a	to chase	**ricordare a**	to remind
dare un calcio a	to kick	**rinunciare a**	to give up
dare un pugno a	to punch	**servire a**	to be good for
fare attenzione a	to pay attention	**stringere la mano a**	to shake hands with
fare bene (male)	to be good (bad)	**tenere a**	to care about
fare piacere a	to please		

B. Before an Infinitive

abituarsi a	to get used to	**insegnare a**	to teach
affrettarsi a	to hurry	**invitare a**	to invite to
aiutare a	to help	**mandare a**	to send
cominciare a	to begin	**obbligare a**	to oblige
continuare a	to continue	**pensare a**	to think about
convincere a	to convince	**persuadere a**	to convince
costringere a	to compel	**preparare a**	to prepare
decidersi a	to make up	**provare a**	to try one's mind
divertirsi a	to have a good time	**rinunciare a**	to give up
fare meglio a	to be better off	**riprendere a**	to resume
fare presto a	to do fast	**riuscire a**	to succeed
imparare a	to learn	**sbrigarsi a**	to hurry
incoraggiare a	to encourage	**servire a**	to be good for

a + verbs of movement:

andare a	to go
correre a	to run
fermarsi a	to stop
passare a	to stop by
stare a	to stay
tornare a	to return
venire a	to come

6. Verbs and Expressions Followed by the Preposition *di*

A. Before a Noun or Pronoun

accorgersi di	to notice, realize	**nutrirsi di**	to feed on
avere bisogno di	to need	**occuparsi di**	to plan
avere paura di	to be afraid	**pensare di**	to have an opinion about
dimenticarsi di	to forget	**preoccuparsi di**	to worry about
fidarsi di	to trust	**ricordarsi di**	to remember
innamorarsi di	to fall in love	**ridere di**	to laugh at
interessarsi di	to be interested in	**soffrire di**	to suffer from
lamentarsi di	to complain	**trattare di**	to deal with
meravigliarsi di	to be surprised	**vivere di**	to live on

B. Before an Infinitive

accettare di	to accept	**finire di**	to finish
ammettere di	to admit	**ordinare di**	to order
aspettare di	to wait for	**pensare di**	to plan
augurare di	to wish	**permettere di**	to permit
avere bisogno di	to need	**pregare di**	to beg
cercare di	to try	**proibire di**	to prohibit
chiedere di	to ask	**promettere di**	to promise
confessare di	to confess	**proporre di**	to propose
consigliare di	to advise	**ringraziare di**	to thank
contare di	to plan	**sapere di**	to know
credere di	to believe	**smettere di**	to stop
decidere di	to decide	**sperare di**	to hope
dimenticare di	to forget	**suggerire di**	to suggest
dubitare di	to doubt	**tentare di**	to attempt
fingere di	to pretend	**vietare di**	to avoid

7. Verbs Followed by the Preposition *Su*

contare su	to count on	**riflettere su**	to ponder on
giurare su	to swear on	**scommettere su**	to bet on

8. Verbs Followed Directly by the Infinitive

amare	to love	**piacere**	to like
desiderare	to wish	**potere**	to be able
dovere	to have to, must	**preferire**	to prefer
fare	to make	**sapere**	to know how
gradire	to appreciate	**volere**	to want
lasciare	to let, allow		

9. Impersonal Verbs

basta	it is enough	**pare**	it seems
bisogna	it is necessary		

Note: These verbs may be followed directly by an infinitive.

10. Practice

Rewrite in English.

1. Impariamo a sciare _____

2. Comincio a capire _____

3. Ho dimenticato di studiare _____

4. Penso di venire _____

5. Ha bisogno di studiare _____

6. Pensava a te _____

7. Staremo a casa _____

8. Torneranno a Roma _____

9. Ho paura di tutto _____

10. Aspettano di venire _____

11. Ho bisogno di te _____

12. Lei continua a mangiare _____

13. Insegnava a guidare _____

14. Sperate di vedere _____

15. Mi accorgo di essere in ritardo _____

16. Si innamora di tutti _____

17. Non mi fido di lui _____

18. Lei vive di amore _____

19. Smetti di parlare! _____

20. Contate su vostra sorella _____

21. Ha tentato di camminare _____

22. Finge di guardare nel libro _____

23. Ridiamo di lui _____

24. Ringraziano di tutto _____

11. Practice

Rewrite in Italian.

1. I go dancing   _____

2. We go study   _____

3. Have you (s.) been to Rome?   _____

4. I believe in ghosts   _____

5. They think about vacation   _____

6. I will try to come   _____

7. We are thinking of going   _____

8. I'll teach you to swim   _____

9. I finish working   _____

10. She feels like eating chocolate   _____

11. I begin to speak   _____

12. He stops in Paris   _____

13. We try to come   _____

14. Call me before you leave   _____

15. You (s.) continue to study   _____

16. They promised to go   _____

17. I promised to come   _____

18. They need to think   _____

19. You (pl.) hope to sleep   _____

20. They feel like traveling   _____

21. Stop (s.) talking!   _____

22. They pay attention to the teacher   _____

Chapter 12

Final Review of Verbs

This extra opportunity for review will reinforce your command of the kinds of conjugations you have learned throughout the book, while giving you the chance to use verbs in complete sentences. For each of the exercises, rewrite the sentence(s) in Italian with the correct tense of the verb indicated.

-are Verbs

abitare: to live, to inhabit, to occupy

1. Where do you live? I live in Naples. _____

2. They have lived in Italy for a long time. _____

3. When I was young I lived in Florida._____

4. He would like to live in a big house. _____

5. She hopes to live near the sea. _____

addormentare: to put to sleep, to sleep, to be boring, to make sleepy

6. This movie puts me to sleep. _____

7. It is a boring book. _____

8. This lesson makes me sleepy._____

9. I fall asleep with the light on._____

addormentarsi: to fall asleep, to go to sleep

10. Paul falls asleep in front of the television. _____

11. Don't fall asleep at the movie. _____

12. The child fell asleep right away._____

alzare (qualche cosa): to lift, to raise, to build

13. Please raise the heat; I am cold. _____

14. He should raise his voice; nobody can hear him._____

alzarsi: to get up, to rise, to get tall

15. The young man gets up late all the time. _____

16. The sun rises late in winter. _____

andare: to go, to drive, to fly, to have to, to be needed

17. They go to school at eight o'clock. _____

18. Where did you go last night? _____

19. I would like her to go to college. _____

20. She drove to Rome with me. _____

21. In March we'll fly to Italy. _____

andare a: to go to

22. I am not going to school this evening. _____

23. Would you like to go dancing? _____

24. Next month I will go to visit some friends. _____

25. Could you go to the post office? _____

26. Next week I will go to the museum. _____

27. She would like to go skiing with us. _____

andare da + article: to go to

28. She went to the doctor. _____

29. I would like to go to the butcher. _____

30. I think they went to their friend. _____

andare in: to go to, to go in, to go by

31. Next year I would like to go to Italy. _____

32. She will go to China with some friends. _____

33. Will they go by car or by plane? _____

34. My mom went in the kitchen. _____

arrivare: to arrive

35. My friends will arrive tomorrow. _____

36. Your ticket arrived yesterday. _____

37. I hope they arrived well. _____

arrivare a: to arrive at (place or city)

38. They have arrived at the airport. _____

39. I will arrive in Venice in a week. _____

arrivare in: to arrive (country singular), means of transportation

40. They arrived in America by boat. _____

41. She said she has arrived in China. _____

42. I would like to arrive in Greece in summer. _____

43. I will arrive tomorrow by car. _____

arrivare in: to arrive in (country plural)

44. We arrived in the United States. _____

45. The tourists arrive in summer. _____

aspettare: to wait for

46. I am waiting for my sister. _____

47. I waited for him for a long time. _____

chiamare: to call, to call for, to send for

48. They called a cab an hour ago. _____

49. She is very ill; we must call a doctor. _____

50. They want to phone her, but it is too late. _____

chiamarsi: to be named, to call oneself

51. I don't know what your name is. _____

52. What is your sister's name? Her name is Carla. _____

dare: to give, to pay, to set, to award, to give off, to show, to lend, to take

53. I gave him a book. _____

54. She hoped they would award him the first prize. _____

55. Could you lend me your car on Saturday? _____

56. The president handed in his resignation. _____

57. She gave me a lot of money. _____

desiderare: to wish for, to want, to need, would like

58. The boy wishes for many gifts at Christmas. _____

59. Carlo wants to talk to you. _____

60. Is there anything you need to see? _____

61. At the restaurant she wanted to taste everything. _____

62. Would you like a cup of coffee or tea? _____

63. We want you to come to visit us. _____

diventare: to become, to get, to grow, to make

64. Carla has grown very tall. _____

65. Verdi became very famous. _____

66. People in Italy are getting very old. _____

67. She has become a beautiful girl. _____

fare: to do, to make, to have, to cook, to bake, to walk, to perform

68. What do you suggest that I do? _____

69. She bakes cookies every day. _____

70. She made a beautiful dress. _____

71. I would like to be a teacher. _____

72. Yesterday it was very cold. _____

73. In summer it is very hot. _____

74. I hope you will have a nice vacation. _____

75. They are building a new road. _____

76. He hoped to go for a long walk. _____

77. The artist made a beautiful statue. _____

guardare: to look at/down/forward/after, to watch, to stare, to guard

78. The teacher looks at him. _____

79. Did you look over her homework? _____

80. He was staring at me. _____

mandare: to send

81. She sends the children to bed. _____

82. She sent the children to bed. _____

83. I will send the package right away. _____

84. I hoped you would send me your book. _____

85. You must send the book by mail. _____

86. I am sending you a kiss. _____

pensare: to think, to imagine, to guess

87. I think it is too cold to go out. _____

88. Guess who I saw last night? _____

89. They should have thought about it. _____

sognare: to dream, to imagine

90. I dreamed I was flying. _____

91. Giovanna was daydreaming. _____

92. I would have never imagined winning the lottery. _____

stare: to stay, to be, to be located, to live

93. The children want to stay inside today. _____

94. I will stay in Italy for two weeks._____

95. Kids, be quiet. _____

96. My mother was at the window. _____

97. My friends live in Rome. _____

-ere Verbs

accendere: to light, to turn on

1. Turn on the light, please. _____

2. I do not want you to light a cigarette._____

avere: to have, to feel, to wear

3. Her son has the flu. _____

4. Their relatives do not have any money to live._____

5. I would have done it, if I had had time. _____

6. They used to have many friends. _____

7. Are you hungry? Yes, I am very hungry. _____

8. That boy is very lucky._____

9. My girlfriend is always in a hurry. _____

10. The lady was wearing a beautiful dress. _____

bere: to drink

11. That man drinks too much. _____

12. Let us drink to our health. _____

13. I think he likes to drink red wine. _____

chiedere: to ask for, to charge, to take

14. She asked me for help._____

15. My mother always asks about you. _____

16. How much do you charge for this house? _____

chiudere: to close, to shut, to turn off

17. The shops close at 7:30. _____

18. You never shut the door. _____

19. Did you close the bottle? _____

20. She shut him out of the house. _____

conoscere: to know, to be familiar, to meet

21. Your father knows Italy well. _____

22. Do you know a good doctor? _____

23. I met my husband in Africa. _____

24. I did not know her very well. _____

correre: to run, to go fast, to rush

25. That boy was running like the wind. _____

26. The train runs fast. _____

27. We must run to get the bus. _____

28. Kids cannot run at the pool. _____

credere a, in: to believe in

29. Nobody believes him. _____

30. Paul does not believe in God. _____

credere che: to believe, to think that

31. I did not believe they had already arrived. _____

32. He believes it will rain tomorrow. _____

decidere di: to decide, to resolve to

33. I cannot decide when to go to Italy. _____

34. He decided to respect the rules. _____

35. They will decide soon where to go on vacation. _____

difendere: to defend, to plead, to protect

36. She always defends her brother. _____

37. The soldiers defended the town. _____

38. The gloves protect your hands from the cold. _____

dispiacere: to regret, to mind

39. Would you mind if I came home with you? _____

40. I regret not being able to visit you. _____

41. If you don't mind, I would like to rest. _____

42. I am sorry that your mother could not come. _____

dovere: must, to need to, ought to, to have to

43. What should I do? _____

44. I should not tell you this story. _____

45. Carlo was to become a great writer. _____

46. You do not need to buy it today. _____

essere: to be, to exist, to happen

47. Where are you from? Are you American? _____

48. What time is it? Is it early, or is it late? _____

49. Paolo is not at home. _____

50. What will be, will be. _____

51. It is not possible that they will come. _____

52. It was not possible for them to come. _____

53. What happened? _____

mettere: to put, to place, to stick, to hang

54. We put all the books on the desk. _____

55. We have hung the curtains. _____

56. Have you put away the suitcases? _____

mettersi: to place, to put on oneself

57. She put on her new bathing suit. _____

58. She started to cry._____

59. He placed himself near the window. _____

nascere: to be born, to rise, to sprout

60. My son was born on October 12._____

61. Do you think that I was born yesterday? _____

62. Your sister was born in Venice. _____

63. The sun rises in the East. _____

64. They sprout like mushrooms._____

rispondere: to answer, to reply, to respond

65. I hope you will answer my letter. _____

66. Why didn't you answer my question? _____

67. Nobody answers the phone. _____

rispondere di: to be responsible for, to vouch for

68. The kids have to pay for the broken glass._____

69. She is responsible for his actions. _____

scrivere: to write, to spell, to say

70. How is your last name spelled? _____

71. Should I type the letter? _____

72. She has written to the Italian consulate._____

73. Dante wrote a lot in his life. _____

74. She hopes you will write her soon. _____

75. I wrote him not to come. _____

tenere: to keep, to hold, to hold on to, to hold back, to have, to occupy

76. The little boy was holding a toy in his hand. _____

77. The police were holding the people back. _____

78. I kept the water in the refrigerator. _____

79. May I keep my coat on? I am cold. _____

80. She wants to keep the windows closed. _____

vedere: to see, to show

81. Have you seen a good movie? _____

82. I would like to see him happy. _____

83. I cannot wait to leave for Italy. _____

84. Does the stain still show? _____

85. We saw a star falling. _____

86. He will go to see his mother. _____

87. They used to go to see him ski. _____

vendere: to sell

88. He sells books. _____

89. She has sold many houses. _____

90. They sell wholesale. _____

91. I do not like to sell. _____

volere: to want to, to refuse to, to mean to

92. They would like to travel, but they cannot. _____

93. Today my car refuses to work. _____

94. She does not want you to come tomorrow. _____

95. I wish you would tell her. _____

96. She wants to study Italian. _____

97. We want to see your paintings. _____

98. He wants to buy a new car. _____

-ire Verbs

aprire: to open, to start, to turn on

1. Open the door, please. _____

2. He wants to open a checking account. _____

3. Do not turn on the television. _____

4. The band was leading the parade. _____

aprirsi: to open, to bloom

5. The spring flowers have bloomed. _____

6. The windows in the apartment open to the sea. _____

7. School opens in the fall. _____

costruire: to build, to construct

8. They are building a new highway. _____

9. I hope to build a new house. _____

10. With hard work, you can build a fortune. _____

dire: to say, to tell, to speak, to express

11. Young children often tell lies. _____

12. His father told him so. _____

13. She told them to call us when they arrive. _____

14. I hope you did not say anything. _____

15. Tell him the truth! _____

16. The witness declared that he had not seen the accident. _____

divertire: to amuse, to entertain

17. Cartoons entertain children. _____

18. The lady has fun with the children. _____

divertirsi: to enjoy oneself, to have fun

19. Did you enjoy yourself in New York? _____

20. Have fun! _____

21. That child has fun playing with Legos. _____

22. I do not have fun at the circus. _____

finire: to end, to finish, to be done, to stop

23. I already know how the book ends. _____

24. The lesson ends at 9:00 P.M. _____

25. Are you done? _____

26. Did you spend all the money? _____

27. The ice cream is all gone. _____

28. I did not finish my homework. _____

partire: to depart, to leave, to take off

29. They departed by plane for Italy. _____

30. My friends left yesterday for the beach. _____

31. The train takes off at exactly 10:00 A.M. _____

32. I will leave on Tuesday. _____

33. They left early. _____

preferire: to prefer, to like better

34. My mother likes coffee better than tea. _____

35. I would rather read than watch television. _____

36. I prefer that you stay inside. _____

37. They prefer downhill skiing to skating. _____

pulire: to clean

38. Every Friday I clean my house. _____

39. Clean your shoes before you come in. _____

40. Clean your nose. _____

salire: to go, to come up, to climb, to ascend, to rise

41. The spacecraft was rising very fast. _____

42. You have to come up to the third floor. _____

43. The price of fruit has gone up again. _____

44. She has to get on the bus. _____

45. My daughter went up with the elevator. _____

sentire: to hear, to listen, to know

46. The mother heard the baby cry. _____

47. Did you listen to the concert? _____

48. I would like to know your opinion. _____

49. My grandfather does not hear well. _____

soffrire: to suffer, to stand, to bear

50. Giovanna has been suffering from a headache. _____

51. They suffered from hunger. _____

52. The orange trees have suffered from the frost. _____

spedire: to mail, to ship

53. I will mail you a letter. _____

54. They shipped you a big box. _____

55. I would like to mail you a gift. _____

uscire: to leave, to go out, to get out, to lead

56. Your father went out on foot. _____

57. My friends left half an hour ago. _____

58. Do not go out. It is raining. _____

venire: to come

59. Would you like to come with us? _____

60. They came to Italy many years ago. _____

61. I think someone is coming. _____

62. At what time did you come home? _____

63. Where does that girl come from? _____

64. This oil comes from the farm. _____

65. The snow was coming down slowly. _____

Answer Key

Chapter 1

Page 5, Practice 8

1. canto, canti, canta, cantiamo, cantate, cantano
2. provo, provi, prova, proviamo, provate, provano
3. lavoro, lavori, lavora, lavoriamo, lavorate, lavorano
4. ricordo, ricordi, ricorda, ricordiamo, ricordate, ricordano
5. viaggio, viaggi, viaggia, viaggiamo, viaggiate, viaggiano
6. volo, voli, vola, voliamo, volate, volano

Page 6, Practice 9

Io:	studio, insegno, viaggio, salto
Tu:	parli, mangi, trovi, balli
Lui, Lei:	impara, entra, lava, riposa
Noi:	compriamo, arriviamo, aiutiamo, tagliamo
Voi:	parlate, imparate, aspettate, pensate
Loro:	spiegano, insegnano, contano, camminano

Page 7, Practice 10

1. mangiamo, 2. impara, 3. comprano, 4. canto, 5. cammini, 6. parlate, 7. studiamo, 8. cambia, 9. pensate, 10. nuota, 11. gioco, 12. pranziamo, 13. viaggiate, 14. ballano, 15. lavora, 16. laviamo, 17. penso, 18. impariamo, 19. ascolto, 20. ama, 21. abitate, 22. pagano, 23. entri, 24. ispezioniamo, 25. pensa, 26. mandi

Page 8, Practice 11

1. we eat, 2. I learn, 3. they buy, 4. I sing, 5. you (s.) walk, 6. you (pl.) speak, 7. we study, 8. I change, 9. you (pl.) think, 10. I swim, 11. I play, 12. we have lunch, 13. you (pl.) travel, 14. they dance, 15. he/she works, 16. we wash, 17. I think, 18. we learn, 19. I listen, 20. he/she loves, 21. you (pl.) live, 22. they pay, 23. you (s.) enter, 24. we inspect, 25. he/she thinks, 26. you (s.) send

Page 9, Practice 12

1. mangio, 2. pensi, 3. imparano, 4. cantiamo, 5. mangiate, 6. lui studia, 7. lei insegna, 8. imparo, 9. lavori, 10. lavano, 11. lei entra, 12. riposiamo, 13. aspetti, 14. cantano, 15. ballo, 16. saltiamo, 17. viaggio, 18. lui trova, 19. arriviamo, 20. aspettate, 21. lei aiuta, 22. compro, 23. lei trova, 24. studiamo

Negative and Interrogative Forms

1. non mangio, 2. non lavori, 3. non ricordiamo, 4. non lavorano, 5. non entra, 6. io non riposo, 7 mangi?, 8. lavori?, 9. ricordiamo?, 10. lavorano?, 11. entra?, 12. riposo?

Page 10, Practice 13

1. we speak, 2. you (s.) jump, 3. he/she thinks, 4. you (pl.) sing, 5. I play, 6. we eat, 7. they learn, 8. you (s.) find, 9. we enter, 10. you (s.) work, 11. we teach, 12. you (pl.) wash, 13. I rest, 14. he/she looks, 15. we walk, 16. you (pl.) bring, 17. you (s.) dance, 18. they speak, 19. he/she travels, 20. we help, 21. I remember, 22. he/she forgets, 23. I don't eat, 24. they don't walk, 25. you (pl.) don't work, 26. do you (s.) work?

Page 12, Practice 15

1. do, dai, dà, diamo, date, danno
2. faccio, fai, fa, facciamo, fate, fanno
3. sto, stai, sta, stiamo, state, stanno
4. vado, vai, va, andiamo, andate, vanno

Chapter 2

Page 15, Practice 3

1. divido, dividi, divide, dividiamo, dividete, dividono
2. chiudo, chiudi, chiude, chiudiamo, chiudete, chiudono
3. metto, metti, mette, mettiamo, mettete, mettono
4. convinco, convinci, convince, convinciamo, convincete, convincono
5. spingo, spingi, spinge, spingiamo, spingete, spingono
6. perdo, perdi, perde, perdiamo, perdete, perdono

Page 16, Practice 4

Io: apprendo, attendo, chiedo, chiudo
Tu: cadi, confondi, dividi, cresci
Lui, Lei: decide, difende, discute, conclude
Noi: apprendiamo, attendiamo, insistiamo, esistiamo
Voi: cadete, ridete, rispondete, nascondete
Loro: perdono, piangono, insistono, promettono

Page 17, Practice 5

1. temo, 2. attendi, 3. cade, 4. chiediamo, 5. assisti, 6. chiude, 7. confondono, 8. conosci, 9. decidono, 10. difende, 11. discute, 12. decidiamo, 13. chiede, 14. godi, 15. concludo, 16. insiste, 17. mettiamo, 18. perde, 19. prometto, 20. promettiamo, 21. piangiamo, 22. rispondono, 23. vedo, 24. vede, 25. scrivo, 26. piango

Negative and Interrogative Forms

1. non assisto, 2. non attendi, 3. non chiediamo, 4. non dividono, 5. non chiude, 6. non piange, 7. assisti?, 8. attendi?, 9. chiedi?, 10. dividono?, 11. chiudi?, 12. piangi?

Page 18, Practice 6

1. we learn, 2. he/she fears, 3. we assume, 4. they attend, 5. I fall, 6. you (pl.) believe, 7. he/she asks, 8. they close, 9. you (s.) correct, 10. you (pl.) conclude, 11. they share, 12. they confuse, 13. you (s.) know, 14. they know, 15. you (pl.) cook, 16. he/she cooks, 17. I decide, 18. you (pl.) defend, 19. we discuss, 20. we include, 21. he/she insists, 22. you (pl.) lose, 23. they lose, 24. they cry, 25. he/she pretends, 26. you (s.) answer, 27. I see, 28. you (s.) win, 29. he/she knows, 30. they win, 31. you (pl.) laugh, 32. they break, 33. I don't stay, 34. they don't allow, 35. we don't read, 36. do you (pl.) read?, 37. do you (s.) read?, 38. do we see?, 39. does he/she write?, 40. do they fear?, 41. don't you (pl.) see?, 42. don't you (s.) read?, 43. don't they write?, 44. don't we write?

Page 20, Practice 8

1. devo, devi, deve, dobbiamo, dovete, devono
2. scelgo, scegli, sceglie, scegliamo, scegliete, scelgono
3. posso, puoi, può, possiamo, potente, possono
4. so, sai, sa, sappiamo, sapete, sanno
5. tengo, tieni, tiene, teniamo, tenete, tengono
6. voglio, vuoi, vogliamo, volete, vogliono

Page 23, Practice 10

1. avverto, avverti, avverte, avvertiamo, avvertite, avvertono
2. bollo, bolli, bolle, bolliamo, bollite, bollono
3. sento, senti, sente, sentiamo, sentite, sentono
4. capisco, capisci, capisce, capiamo, capite, capiscono
5. preferisco, preferisci, preferisce, preferiamo, preferite, preferiscono

Page 24, Practice 11

Io:	apro, capisco, offro, finisco
Tu:	dormi, avverti, bolli, senti
Lui, Lei:	preferisce, parte, veste, spedisce
Noi:	serviamo, vestiamo, apriamo, capiamo
Voi:	avvertite, seguite, costruite, istruite
Loro:	sentono, inseguono, investono, partono

Page 25, Practice 12

1. preferisco, 2. acconsenti, 3. copre, 4. godiamo, 5. fuggono, 6. capisce, 7. segue, 8. menti, 9. sento, 10. soffriamo, 11. aprono, 12. finisce, 13. applaudi, 14. converte, 15. applaudo, 16. dorme, 17. inghiottisco, 18. partite, 19. servono, 20. dormo, 21. preferisce, 22. capisco, 23. preferiamo, 24. costruisco

Negative and Interrogative Forms

1. non finisco, 2. non capisce, 3. non istruiscono, 4. non senti, 5. non dormo, 6. non applaudiamo, 7. non partiamo, 8. non soffro, 9. costruiamo?, 10. sente?, 11. capiscono?, 12. sentono?, 13. dorme?, 14. acconsenti?, 15. finisce?, 16. partiamo?

Page 26, Practice 13

1. you (s.) agree, 2. they applaud, 3. he/she opens, 4. they open, 5. we announce, 6. he/she boils, 7. I understand, 8. you (pl.) consent, 9. they convert, 10. I cover, 11. he/she builds, 12. he/she offers, 13. we enjoy, 14. you (pl.) sleep, 15. they follow, 16. we finish, 17. he/she escapes, 18. you (s.) heal, 19. they guarantee, 20. you (s.) swallow, 21. they chase, 22. he/she instructs, 23. they prefer, 24. you (pl.) follow, 25. you (pl.) clean, 26. they punish, 27. he/she hits, 28. I serve, 29. he/she suffers, 30. I substitute, 31. we send, 32. they substitute, 33. we suggest, 34. they transfer

Negative and Interrogative Forms

1. we don't sleep, 2. he/she doesn't suffer, 3. we don't understand, 4. he/she doesn't instruct, 5. you (s.) don't open, 6. do you (s.) agree?, 7. do they leave?, 8. do you (s.) sleep?, 9. do you (s.) understand?, 10. do you (pl.) clean?

Page 28, Practice 15

1. vengo, vieni, viene, veniamo, venite, vengono
2. dico, dici, dice. diciamo, dite, dicono
3. esco, esci, esce, usciamo, uscite, escono

Page 28, Practice 16

1. dici, 2. escono, 3. veniamo, 4. muoiono, 5. salto, 6. dice, 7. esco, 8. vengono, 9. salgono, 10. usciamo, 11. salite, 12. muore, 13. odi, 14. dicono, 15. udiamo, 16. dite

Chapter 3

Page 30, Practice 3

1. parla, 2. canta, 3. andate, 4. non andare, 5. andiamo, 6. non mangiate, 7. finiamo, 8. non giocate, 9. gioca, 10. guarda, 11. ascolta, 12. non partire, 13. partiamo, 14. giocate, 15. giochiamo, 16. esci, 17. non uscite, 18. gioca, 19. non giocare, 20. mangiate, 21. scrivi, 22. non scrivere, 23. scriviamo, 24. chiudi, 25. non chiudere, 26. chiudiamo, 27. dormi, 28. dormite, 29. bevi, 30. bevete, 31. leggi, 32. leggiamo, 33. non leggere, 34. non leggete

Page 31, Practice 4

1. speak (pl.), 2. sing, 3. don't sing, 4. listen, 5. listen (pl.), 6. let's go, 7. speak, 8. don't speak, 9. let's play, 10. don't play (pl.), 11. go out (pl.), 12. don't go out, 13. eat, 14. let's eat, 15. close, 16. ask (pl.), 17. think, 18. don't think (pl.), 19. suggest, 20. leave, 21. put (pl.), 22. don't put, 23. hope, 24. come in (pl.), 25. study, 26. don't study, 27. don't leave (pl.), 28. sing, 29. let's sing, 30. push, 31. don't push, 32. take (pl.)

Page 33, Practice 7

1. aspetti, 2. aspettino, 3. paghi, 4. paghino, 5. mangi, 6. rispondano, 7. finisca, 8. guardino, 9. venga, 10. mangino, 11. risponda, 12. finiscano, 13. vengano, 14. esca, 15. partino, 16. mi dica, 17. pensi, 18. escano, 19. cammini, 20. cantino, 21. leggano, 22. sorrida

Page 35, Practice 9

1. vedrò, vedrai, vedrà, vedremo, vedrete, vedranno
2. andrò, andrai, andrà, andremo, andrete, andranno
3. capirò, capirai, capirà, capiremo, capirete, capiranno
4. aiuterò, aiuterai, aiuterà, aiuteremo, aiuterete, aiuteranno

Page 36, Practice 10

Io:	parlerò, vedrò, pulirò
Tu:	viaggerai, permetterai, capirai
Lui, Lei:	troverà, saprà, sentirà
Noi:	guarderemo, berremo, finiremo
Voi:	lavorerete, avrete, partirete
Loro:	andranno, saranno, sentiranno

Page 37, Practice 11

1. I'll understand, 2. I'll work, 3. you'll (s.) read, 4. he/she'll sing, 5. you'll (pl.) hear, 6. you'll (s.) plant, 7. I'll listen, 8. you'll (pl.) plant, 9. we'll see, 10. they'll answer, 11. I'll pay, 12. we'll play, 13. you'll (s.) think, 14. you'll (pl.) see, 15. you'll (s.) hear, 16. I'll decide, 17. we'll cry, 18. he/she'll win, 19. you'll (pl.) discuss, 20. we'll go, 21. I'll study, 22. you'll (pl.) think, 23. you'll (s.) write, 24. I'll cook, 25. I'll finish, 26. we'll play, 27. we'll stay, 28. you'll (s.) do/make, 29. you'll (pl.) give, 30. you'll (s.) leave, 31. you'll (pl.) tell, 32. we'll sleep, 33. you'll (s.) chase, 34. we'll come, 35. I'll boil, 36. they'll applaud, 37. he/she'll open, 38. we'll climb

Negative Future Forms
1. I won't eat, 2. we won't go, 3. he/she won't do/make, 4. we won't sing, 5. he/she won't understand, 6. you (pl.) won't finish

Page 38, Practice 12

1. attenderò, 2. cadrà, 3. scriveremo, 4. penseranno, 5. capiremo, 6. chiuderò, 7. parlerai, 8. giocheremo, 9. viaggeranno, 10. metterò, 11. faremo, 12. troverà, 13. troveremo, 14. ascolterò, 15. impareremo, 16. mangerò, 17. andremo, 18. faranno, 19. starò, 20. comprerò, 21. verranno, 22. verrò, 23. guarderemo, 24. diremo, 25. dirà, 26. canteranno, 27. piangeremo, 28. pianterò, 29. usciremo, 30. saliranno, 31. andrete, 32. seguiremo, 33. insisterà, 34. vedrà, 35. risponderemo, 36. pagherò, 37. voteremo, 38. deciderò, 39. berremo, 40. sentiremo

Negative Future Forms
1. non mangerò, 2. non ascolterà, 3. non berremo, 4. non mangeranno

Chapter 4

Page 40, Practice 3

1. pensavo, pensavi, pensava, pensavamo, pensavate, pensavano
2. bevevo, bevevi, beveva, bevevamo, bevevate, bevevano
3. finivo, finivi, finiva, finivamo, finivate, finivano
4. abitavo, abitavi, abitava, abitavamo, abitavate, abitavano

Page 41, Practice 4

Io:	mangiavo, mettevo, sentivo
Tu:	cantavi, vedevi, finivi
Lui, Lei:	saltava, beveva, apriva
Noi:	votavamo, rispondevamo, costruivamo
Voi:	giocavate, comprendevate, applaudivate
Loro:	speravano, vendevano, preferivano

Page 42, Practice 5

A. 1. parlava, 2. cantavate, 3. abitava, 4. partivamo, 5. giocavate, 6. finivano, 7. camminavo, 8. perdevi, 9. comprendevate, 10. mangiavano, 11. costruivi, 12. istruivate, 13. lavorava, 14. ballava, 14. pensavano, 16. credevate, 17. lavavi, 18. scrivevamo, 19. correvo, 20. parlava

B. **Note:** The imperfect can be translated as **used to** or **was + verb ending in ing.** 1. we used to eat, 2. you (s.) used to study, 3. you (s.) used to drink, 4. you (s.) were playing, 5. he/she was listening, 6. you (pl.) used to understand, 7. they were writing, 8. I was asking, 9. you (pl.) were closing, 10. he/she used to listen, 11. we used to take, 12. I was learning, 13. we used to sell, 14, you (s.) used to sell, 15. you (s.) used to understand, 16. they were living, 17. he/she was instructing, 18. he/she used to see, 19. they were receiving, 20. I was teaching

Page 43, Practice 6

1. mangiavano, 2. pensavamo, 3. venivi, 4. credevo, 5. non pensavano, 6. imparavo, 7. credevano, 8. chiedevamo, 9. non volevi, 10. aspettava, 11. imparavano, 12. capivo, 13. potevi, 14. cantavamo, 15. volevano, 16. pensavo, 17. pensavamo, 18. voleva, 19. andava, 20. aspettavo, 21. speravo, 22. speravamo, 23. parlavo, 24. studiavi?, 25. parlavi?, 26. sperava, 27. pensavi, 28. lavoravamo, 29. volevano, 30. guardavamo, 31. guardavamo?, 32. viaggiava, 33. insegnavo, 34. mangiavano, 35. non capivo, 36. non potevo, 37. cantavano, 38. non volevano, 39. non pensavo, 40. pensavi, 41. voleva, 42. pulivo, 43. guardavamo, 44. non speravano, 45. sperava, 46. dubitavi

Page 44, Practice 9

1. mangiai, mangiasti, mangiò, mangiammo, mangiaste, mangiarono
2. potei, potesti, potè, potemmo, poteste, poterono
3. capii, capisti, capì, capimmo, capiste, capirono

Page 46, Practice 11

Io:	chiesi, conobbi, sentii
Tu:	comprasti, temesti, finisti
Carlo:	nacque, vide, volle
Maria:	capì, scrisse, venne
Noi:	facemmo, bevemmo, ridemmo
Voi:	scendeste, vinceste, metteste
Loro:	offrirono, partirono, fecero

Page 47, Practice 12

1. I came, 2. I laughed, 3. I drank, 4. he fell, 5. she asked, 6. we closed, 7. you (pl.) knew, 8. you (s.) said, 9. she decided, 10. we said, 11. you (pl.) must, 12. they said, 13. I lived, 14. they won, 15. you (s.) did/made, 16. she read, 17. we read, 18. you (s.) put, 19. you (pl.) were born, 20. I took, 21. we took, 22. you (s.) laughed, 23. they laughed, 24. she stayed, 25. you (s.) chose, 26. they wrote, 27. I chose, 28. you (s.) chose, 29. they wrote, 30. you (pl.) stayed, 31. you (s.) saw, 32. we saw, 33. you (pl.) won, 34. I saw, 35. they saw, 36. she lived, 37. he wanted, 38. we wanted, 39. they came, 40. you (s.) stayed

Page 48, Practice 13

1. I speak, 2. we eat, 3. they live, 4. do you (pl.) live?, 5. we drive, 6. I don't work, 7. we'll return, 8. they'll return, 9. I don't fly, 10. do you (pl.) fly?, 11. they'll arrive, 12. I'll arrive, 13. you won't (pl.) arrive, 14. I ask, 15. I wasn't asking, 16. they close, 17. do you (s.) close?, 18. I think, 19. you'll (s.) think, 20. we rest, 21. they rest, 22. you (s.) don't rest, 23. I spoke, 24. we thought, 25. do you (s.) rest?, 26. eat!, 27. look (pl.)!, 28. speak!, 29. learn!, 30. don't look!, 31. don't sleep!, 32. listen (formal)!, 33. do you (s.) promise?, 34. I'll answer, 35. we'll write, 36. I used to read, 37. you (s.) used to speak, 38. you (pl.) wanted, 39. they used to cry, 40. you (s.) used to insist, 41. you (s.) used to drink, 42. drink!, 43. drink! (pl.), 44. don't drink!, 45. you (s.) come, 46. do you (s.) come?, 47. he/she read, 48. you (pl.) heard

1. abitano, 2. aprivo, 3. lavorarono, 4. saliamo, 5. capisco, 6. mangiarono, 7. mangiammo, 8. lavora, 9. studiano, 10. tengo, 11. scrivo, 12. scrivevi, 13. scriverò, 14. viaggi, 15. viaggiavi, 16. viaggeranno, 17. parto, 18. parte, 19. partiremo, 20. partiva, 21. imparava, 22. imparavamo, 23. pensavano, 24. vivrò, 25. apriremo, 26. mangia!, 27. lavora!, 28. mangerà, 29. lavorerà, 30. studia!, 31. studiate!, 32. bevi!, 33. bevete!, 34. promettevamo, 35. volevo, 36. deve, 37. rispondi!, 38. scriva!, 39. aspetti!, 40. dissi, 41. aspetteremo, 42. discuto, 43. vedevamo, 44. sanno, 45. capiamo, 46. pensavo

Chapter 5

Page 56, Practice 7

1. ho mangiato, hai mangiato, ha mangiato, abbiamo mangiato, avete mangiato, hanno mangiato
2. ho scritto, hai scritto, ha scritto, abbiamo scritto, avete scritto, hanno scritto
3. sono venuto/a, sei venuto/a, è venuto/a, siamo venuti/e, siete venuti/e, sono venuti/e
4. sono andato/a, sei andato/a, è andato/a, siamo andati/e, siete andati/e, sono andati/e

Page 57, Practice 8

Io:	ho mangiato	ho visto	ho sentito
Tu:	hai parlato	hai scritto	hai capito
Lui:	ha viaggiato	ha potuto	ha finito
Lei:	ha camminato	ha voluto	è venuta
Noi:	abbiamo lodato	abbiamo spinto	siamo saliti/e
Voi:	siete stati/e	avete riso	avete aperto
Loro:	hanno dato	sono rimasti/e	hanno nutrito
Carlo:	ha fatto	è nato	ha offerto
Maria:	è andata	ha nascosto	ha pulito
Io e Giovanni:	abbiamo aspettato	abbiamo venduto	siamo partiti
Tu e Pietro:	avete imparato	avete chiuso	siete usciti
Giovanni e Paolo:	hanno fermato	hanno vissuto	hanno finito

Page 58, Practice 9

Io:	non sono stato/a	non ho avuto	non ho potuto
Tu:	non hai voluto	non hai dovuto	non hai capito
Lui:	non ha fatto	non ha dato	non è stato
Noi:	non siamo andati/e	non siamo arrivati/e	non siamo partiti/e

Page 59, Practice 10

1. ha parlato, 2. siamo stati/e, 3. è stata, 4. avete letto, 5. hanno sentito, 6. ho dormito, 7. hai perso, 8. è andata, 9. ha deciso, 10. abbiamo comprato, 11. avete vissuto, 12. hanno bevuto, 13. ha parlato, 14. ha aperto, 15. ha aperto, 16. avete imparato, 17. abbiamo temuto, 18. ho mangiato, 19. hai ricevuto, 20. ha lavorato, 21. abbiamo viaggiato, 22. hanno potuto, 23. avete insegnato, 24. abbiamo sciato, 25. abbiamo corso, 26. ho guardato, 27. hai guarito, 28. avete risposto, 29. sono arrivati/e, 39. abbiamo tenuto, 31. ha venduto, 32. hanno vissuto, 33. ho abitato, 34. abbiamo gettato

Page 59, Practice 11

1. non ha mangiato, 2. non ha comprato, 3. non hai parlato, 4. non ho studiato, 5. non hanno dovuto, 6. non abbiamo cantato, 7. non hanno visto, 8. non avete sentito, 9. non hai scritto, 10. non abbiamo voluto

Page 60, Practice 12

1. abbiamo risposto, 2. hanno comprato, 3. abbiamo imparato, 4. ha comprato, 5. ho chiesto, 6. hai risposto, 7. abbiamo lasciato, 8. ho bevuto, 9. non ho bevuto, 10. hanno insegnato, 11. ho letto, 12. hai scritto, 13. hanno lavorato, 14. ha dormito, 15. ha lavorato, 16. abbiamo studiato, 17. non ha sciato, 18. non è andata, 19. è nata, 20. hanno venduto, 21. non ho ascoltato, 22. non ho sentito, 23. non ho chiesto, 24. non hai risposto, 25. ho ricevuto, 26. ho imparato, 27. hanno capito, 28. ha viaggiato, 29. non abbiamo viaggiato, 30. hanno pulito, 31. abbiamo pensato, 32. non hanno pensato, 33. ho pulito, 34. hai pagato, 35. non hai pagato, 36. abbiamo mangiato, 37. sono arrivato/a, 38. sono stati/e

Page 61, Practice 15

1. avevo guardato, avevi guardato, aveva guardato, avevamo guardato, avevate guardato, avevano guardato
2. avevo visto, avevi visto, aveva visto, avevamo visto, avevate visto, avevano visto
3. ero partito/a, eri partito/a, era partito/a, eravamo partiti/e, eravate partiti/e, erano partiti/e

Page 62, Practice 16

Io:	avevo mangiato	avevo visto	avevo sentito
Tu:	avevi parlato	avevi creduto	avevi pulito
Lui, Lei:	aveva visitato	aveva scritto	aveva finito
Noi:	eravamo arrivati/e	avevamo bevuto	avevamo capito
Voi:	avevate comprato	avevate letto	eravate venuti/e
Loro:	avevano dato	avevano potuto	avevano aperto
Carlo:	aveva giocato	aveva spinto	aveva costruito
Carlo e Maria:	avevano viaggiato	avevano venduto	erano partiti

Page 63, Practice 17

1. avevo capito, 2. eri andato/a, 3. aveva studiato, 4. aveva bevuto, 5. avevamo finito, 6. avevate dormito, 7. avevano comprato, 8. avevo lavorato, 9. avevi pensato, 10. aveva giocato, 11. avevamo viaggiato, 12. avevate pulito, 13. avevano guardato, 14. ero stato/a, 15. eri arrivato/a, 16. era partito, 17. era andata, 18. avevamo letto, 19. avevate scritto, 20. avevamo finito, 21. avevo vinto, 22. aveva perso, 23. era andata, 24. avevamo ascoltato

Page 64, Practice 18

1. ho mangiato, 2. avevi mangiato, 3. è andata, 4. era venuto, 5. abbiamo finito, 6. avevamo finito, 7. avete visto, 8. avevate guardato, 9. hanno letto, 10. avevano letto, 11. ho giocato, 12. avevo dormito, 13. ha mangiato, 14. avevamo sciato, 15. non abbiamo letto, 16. non avevamo pensato, 17. non hanno vinto, 18. non avevamo promesso, 19. non ho scelto, 20. non è venuto, 21. non era partita, 22. abbiamo vissuto, 23. non abbiamo vissuto, 24. avevamo vissuto

Chapter 6

Page 66, Practice 3

1. andrei, andresti, andrebbe, andremmo, andreste, andrebbero
2. dovrei, dovresti, dovrebbe, dovremmo, dovreste, dovrebbero
3. verrei, verresti, verrebbe, verremmo, verreste, verrebbero

Page 67, Practice 4

Io:	canterei	potrei	capirei
Tu:	balleresti	vedresti	dormiresti
Lui, Lei:	nuoterebbe	berrebbe	sentirebbe
Noi:	ordineremmo	leggeremmo	finiremmo
Voi:	viaggereste	dovreste	partireste
Loro:	domanderebbero	vorrebbero	verrebbero
Giovanna:	ascolterebbe	avrebbe	direbbe
Io e Carlo:	parleremmo	vedremmo	colpiremmo
Tu e Giovanna:	desiderereste	vincereste	ubbidireste
Giovanna e Carlo:	organizzerebbero	prometterebbero	offrirebbero

Page 68, Practice 5

Io:	non parlerei	non vedrei	non sentirei
Tu:	non viaggeresti	non scriveresti	non puliresti
Paolo:	non mangerebbe	non potrebbe	non capirebbe
Io e Carlo:	non studieremmo	non leggeremmo	non finiremmo
Tu e Paolo:	non arrivereste	non vorreste	non partireste

Page 69, Practice 6

1. I would buy, 2. you (s.) would see, 3. I would understand, 4. we wouldn't eat, 5. you (pl.) would come, 6. they would hear, 7. I would study, 8. I wouldn't study, 9. you (s.) would travel, 10. he/she would understand, 11. Carla would arrive, 12. we would be, 13. they would write, 14. I would sleep, 15. you (s.) wouldn't read, 16. Paolo wouldn't leave, 17. we would make/do, 18. you (pl.) would not play, 19. you (pl.) would be, 20. they would listen, 21. I would come, 22. I wouldn't come, 23. you (s.) would stay, 24. Carlo would understand, 25. Maria would cook, 26. we would play, 27. we would want, 28. we wouldn't want, 29. you and Paolo would do/make, 30. I wouldn't do/make, 31. we would go, 32. you (pl.) would bring, 33. Carla couldn't bring, 34. they should, 35. I would invite, 36. they would come

Interrogative Forms

1. would you (s.) come?, 2. would they sing?, 3. would he/she understand?, 4. would you (pl.) give?, 5. would he/she speak?, 6. would you (s.) listen?, 7. would we make/do?, 8. would you (s.) cook?

Page 70, Practice 7

1. penserei, 2. berrei, 3. potresti, 4. farebbe, 5. non farebbe, 6. scriverebbe, 7. lavorerei, 8. berrebbero, 9. pulirei, 10. farebbe, 11. laverebbero, 12. guarderei, 13. vedrebbero, 14. penseremmo, 15. laverei, 16. capiresti, 17. non andrebbero, 18. vedreste, 19. non prenderei, 20. saprei, 21. andresti, 22. non potresti, 23. penserebbe, 24. scriveremmo, 25. leggerebbero, 26. dormirei, 27. non potrebbero, 28. mangeremmo, 29. berrei, 30. viaggereste, 31. ritornerebbe, 32. arriverebbe, 33. partirebbero, 34. non arriverei, 35. non pianterebbe, 36. vincerebbe, 37. mangerebbero, 38. nuoteremmo, 39. sciereste, 40. guarderemmo

Page 70, Practice 8

1. dovrei andare, 2. dovresti scrivere, 3. dovrebbero studiare, 4. dovremmo venire, 5. dovrebbe cucinare, 6. dovrebbe leggere

Page 71, Practice 11

1. avrei parlato, avresti parlato, avrebbe parlato, avremmo parlato, avreste parlato, avrebbero parlato
2. avrei visto, avresti visto, avrebbe visto, avremmo visto, avreste visto, avrebbero visto
3. sarei venuto/a, saresti venuto/a, sarebbe venuto/a, saremmo venuti/e, sareste venuti/e, sarebbero venuti/e

Page 72, Practice 12

Io:	sarei andato/a	sarei ritornato/a	sarei partito/a
Tu:	avresti parlato	avresti venduto	avresti capito
Lui, Lei:	sarebbe arrivato/a	avrebbe scritto	avrebbe dormito
Noi:	avremmo informato	avremmo letto	avremmo preferito
Voi:	avreste aspettato	avreste dovuto	avreste finito
Loro:	avrebbero abitato	avrebbero bevuto	sarebbero usciti/e
Carlo:	avrebbe invitato	avrebbe voluto	avrebbe sentito

Page 73, Practice 13

1. I would have waited, 2. you (s.) would talk, 3. he/she would have eaten, 4. they would understand, 5. you (pl.) would write, 6. you (pl.) would have written, 7. they would answer, 8. he/she would not have answered, 9. I would hear, 10. I would have heard, 11. we would have signed, 12. I would invite, 13. you (pl.) would go out, 14. we would finish, 15. they would have finished, 16. you (pl.) would buy, 17. he would buy, 18. you (s.) would find, 19. I would have looked, 20. he/she would answer, 21. he/she would have answered, 22. you (pl.) would have written, 23. I would know, 24. he/she would have known

Page 74, Practice 14

1. andrei, 2. avresti preso, 3. avremmo ballato, 4. sarebbero venuti/e, 5. saprebbe, 6. aspetteremmo, 7. avremmo cominciato, 8. scriverebbe, 9. avrebbe risposto, 10. parlerebbero, 11. sarebbero dovuti/e venire, 12. avrei dovuto parlare, 13. dovrebbe aspettare, 14. avrebbe dovuto aspettare, 15. capiremmo, 16. avrebbero capito, 17. avrebbe scritto, 18. avresti risposto, 19. avresti dovuto rispondere, 20. viaggerebbero, 21. sarei ritornato, 22. sarebbe partito, 23. arriverebbe, 24. partiremmo

Chapter 7

Page 78, Practice 4

1. domandi, domandi, domandi, domandiamo, domandiate, domandino
2. veda, veda, veda, vediamo, vediate, vedano
3. senta, senta, senta, sentiamo, sentiate, sentano
4. capisca, capisca, capisca, capiamo, capiate, capiscano
5. giochi, giochi, giochi, giochiamo, giochiate, giochino
6. paghi, paghi, paghi, paghiamo, paghiate, paghino

Page 79, Practice 5

Che io:	domandi	decida	senta
Che tu:	compri	veda	finisca
Che lui:	prepari	legga	capisca
Che lei:	aspetti	comprenda	pulisca
Che noi:	arriviamo	accendiamo	diciamo
Che voi:	visitiate	beviate	partiate
Che loro:	lavorino	chiudano	capiscano

Page 80, Practice 6

Io voglio che tu:	mangi	legga	parta
Io voglio che lui:	parli	perda	offra
Io voglio che lei:	stia	discuta	apra
Io spero che noi:	impariamo	sorridiamo	capiamo
Io desidero che voi:	facciate	vediate	ridiate
Io penso che loro:	desiderino	debbano	ubbidiscano
Io voglio:	visitare	vincere	capire
Loro vogliono:	visitare	arrivare	partire

Page 81, Practice 7

1. legga, 2. studino, 3. comprino, 4. capisca, 5. venga, 6. arrivino, 7. finisca, 8. venga, 9. possa, 10. legga, 11. veniamo, 12. pensiate, 13. sapere, 14. ritorni, 15. sappia, 16. vada, 17. vinca, 18. perda, 19. pensino, 20. controlli, 21. possano, 22. sapere, 23. puliscano, 24. comprare

Page 82, Practice 8

1. che io vada, 2. che lui senta, 3. che noi mangiamo, 4. che loro parlino, 5. che voi sentiate, 6. che tu beva, 7. che lei parta, 8. che lui capisca, 9. che noi lavoriamo, 10. che voi sentiate, 11. che voi ascoltiate, 12. che loro leggano, 13. che voi non ascoltiate, 14. che voi andiate, 15. che io parta, 16. che lui arrivi, 17. che piova, 18. che io sappia, 19. che tu conosca, 20. che tu possa, 21. che voi non leggiate, 22. che voi compriate, 23. che voi vendiate, 24. che voi capiate

Page 83, Practice 9

1. vada, 2. partire, 3. arrivi, 4. pensi, 5. visiti, 6. andare, 7. capisca, 8. comprare, 9. veda, 10. possa, 11. vogliamo, 12. legga, 13. finire, 14. paghi, 15. ascolti, 16. compri, 17. vendiamo, 18. scriva, 19. guardino, 20. studi, 21. parta, 22. rimaniamo, 23. perdiate, 24. rimanga

Page 85, Practice 12

1. che io ascoltassi, che tu ascoltassi, che lui ascoltasse, che lei ascoltasse, che noi ascoltassimo, che voi ascoltaste, che loro ascoltassero
2. che io conoscessi, che tu conoscessi, che lui conoscesse, che lei conoscesse, che noi conoscessimo, che voi conosceste, che loro conoscessero
3. che io venissi, che tu venissi, che lui venisse, che lei venisse, che noi venissimo, che voi veniste, che loro venissero

Page 86, Practice 13

Che io:	parlassi	leggessi	pulissi
Che tu:	comprassi	vedessi	finissi
Che lui:	andasse	potesse	sentisse
Che lei:	arrivasse	corresse	partisse
Che noi:	dimenticassimo	bevessimo	dormissimo
Che voi:	perdonaste	scriveste	veniste
Che loro:	studiassero	temessero	capissero

Page 87, Practice 14

Pensavo che tu:	facessi	vincessi	capissi
Pensavo che lui:	lavorasse	perdesse	finisse
Pensavo che lei:	studiasse	correggesse	sentisse
Pensavo che noi:	cambiassimo	sapessimo	dormissimo
Pensavo che voi:	sognaste	accendeste	costruiste
Pensavo che loro:	insegnassero	spegnessero	venissero
Speravo che tu:	parlassi	vedessi	finissi
Speravo che voi:	faceste	leggeste	puliste

Page 88, Practice 15

1. volevo che tu venissi, 2. speravo che tu venissi, 3. pensavi di poter studiare, 4. pensavi che lui studiasse, 5. pensavi che venissimo, 6. speravo che voi veniste, 7. credevo che scrivesse, 8. pensavo che andassimo, 9. speravi che chiamassero, 10. pensavano che rimanessi, 11. tutti voi pensavate che giocasse, 12. pensavo che tu pulissi, 13. non sapevo che tu andassi, 14. volevi che io cucinassi, 15. vorrebbe che tu leggessi, 16. sarebbe necessario che tu partissi, 17. mio padre voleva che io lavorassi, 18. era difficile che tu andassi, 19. non sapevo che tu fossi cosí alto/a, 20. voleva che chiedessi al dottore, 21. volevo dormire tutto il giorno, 22. volevo che dormisse tutto il giorno, 23, voleva che andassimo, 24. speravo che mi invitassero

1. parli, 2. parlassi, 3. veniamo, 4. venissimo, 5. sia, 6. fosse, 7. studi, 8. studiasse, 9. studiate, 10. studiaste, 11. venire, 12. venire, 13. impari, 14. imparasse, 15. sogni, 16. sognassi, 17. facciano, 18. facessero, 19. ricordiate, 20. ricordasse, 21. arrivi, 22. arrivasse, 23. scriva, 24. scrivessi

Chapter 8

Page 91, Practice 3

Che io:	sia arrivato/a	abbia visto	abbia finito
Che tu:	abbia parlato	abbia letto	abbia capito
Che lui:	abbia ascoltato	abbia scritto	abbia sentito
Che lei:	abbia piantato	sia scesa	sia salita
Che noi:	abbiamo studiato	abbiamo venduto	abbiamo sostituito
Che voi:	abbiate cancellato	abbiate bevuto	siate venuti/e
Che loro:	abbiano guardato	abbiano mantenuto	siano partiti/e
Che io:	non abbia sperato	non abbia aspettato	non abbia riso

Page 92, Practice 4

1. sia venuto, 2. abbia parlato, 3. abbiamo studiato, 4. abbia perso, 5. siamo andati/e, 6. abbia pagato, 7. abbia arrestato, 8. abbia trovato, 9. abbiate mangiato, 10. sia partita, 11. abbia telefonato, 12. abbiate telefonato, 13. abbia studiato, 14. siano venuti/e, 15. abbiate nuotato, 16. sia ritornato/a, 17. abbia finito, 18. abbia capito, 19. abbia trovato, 20. sia partito, 21. abbia scritto, 22. abbiano studiato, 23. abbia studiato, 24. abbia telefonato

Page 93, Practice 5

1. parli	parlassi	abbia parlato
2. senta	sentissi	abbia sentito
3. capisca	capisse	abbia capito
4. venga	venisse	sia venuta
5. offriamo	offrissimo	abbiamo offerto
6. prendiate	prendeste	aveste preso
7. vedano	vedessero	abbiano visto
8. pensi	pensassi	abbia pensato
9. legga	leggessi	abbia letto
10. pulisca	pulisse	abbia pulito
11. stiamo	stessimo	siamo stati

Page 94, Practice 8

1. That I had arrived
2. That you (s.) had thought
3. That we had left
4. That you (pl.) had spoken
5. That they had come

Page 95, Practice 9

1. Sembrava che avesse saputo tutto, 2. era possibile che fosse arrivata, 3. speravamo che fosse entrata, 4. pensavo che fosse arrivato, 5. dubitavo che avessi saputo, 6. sembrava che avesse capito, 7. era meglio che fossi andato/a, 8. era meglio che fossero partiti/e, 9. sembrava che io avessi saputo, 10. preferivo che foste andati/e, 11. preferivamo che tu avessi studiato, 12. ero sicuro che Carlo fosse arrivato, 13. preferiva che avessimo imparato, 14. ero contento che tu fossi venuto/a, 15. eravamo sicuri che fossero partiti/e, 16. era probabile che fossi arrivato/a, 17. pensavo che tu fossi venuto/a, 18. dubitavo che avesse trovato lavoro, 19. credevo che avesse cercato lavoro, 20. era necessario che io avessi letto, 21. era bene che avessero comprato, 22. era necessario che avessero venduto, 23. speravo che Carlo avesse venduto

1. spiegassi, 2 potessi, 3. avessimo, 4. sapesse, 5. guidasse, 6. avessi spiegato, 7. avesse potuto, 8. avessimo avuto, 9. avesse saputo, 10. avesse guidato, 11. avesse venduto, 12. avessi saputo, 13. avessi potuto, 14. aveste studiato

Page 99, Practice 16

Io:	mi alzo	mi metto	mi sento
Tu:	ti addormenti	ti pettini	ti domandi
Lui:	si lava	si pettina	si veste
Lei:	si diverte	si sposa	si prepara
Noi:	ci vestiamo	ci svegliamo	ci aiutiamo
Voi:	vi parlate	vi salutate	vi incontrate
Loro:	si divertono	si sposano	si preparano

Page 100, Practice 17

1. he wakes up, 2. she gets dressed, 3. they get ready, 4. we get ready, 5. you (pl.) greet each other, 6. they talk to each other, 7. you (pl.) hate each other, 8. they love each other, 9. he/she begins to talk, 10. they write each other, 11. I get up, 12. you wash yourself, 13. he washes himself, 14. Carlo gets dressed, 15. we meet each other, 16. I get dressed, 17. he/she falls asleep, 18. you (pl.) talk to each other, 19. they help each other, 20. I fall asleep, 21. he combs his hair, 22. they look at themselves in the mirror, 23. you (pl.) get ready, 24. they kneel

Page 101, Practice 18

1. ci svegliamo, 2. mi diverto, 3. si alzano, 4. si svegliano, 5. si salutano, 6. si preparano, 7. si lava, 8. si pettina, 9. si incontrano, 10. si divertono, 11. si diverte, 12. si prepara, 13. vi vestite, 14. mi vesto, 15. ci aiutiamo, 16. ci alziamo, 17. ci svegliamo, 18. ci amiamo, 19. ci siamo svegliati, 20. si è alzato, 21. ti sei lavato/a, 22. si è pettinata, 23. si sono odiati/e, 24. si è divertito

Chapter 9

Page 103, Practice 3

A. 1. sto parlando, 2. stai ascoltando, 3 stiamo parlando, 4. sta guidando, 5. sta sentendo, 6. stiamo studiando, 7. state partendo, 8. stai leggendo, 9. sta parlando, 10. sto giocando, 11. stai partendo, 12. stanno tornando

B. 1. stavi andando, 2. stavi ascoltando, 3. stavate parlando, 4. stavo bevendo, 5. stavate vedendo, 6. stavamo giocando, 7. stavate scrivendo, 8. stava leggendo, 9. stavi prendendo, 10. stavo bevendo, 11. stavi partendo, 12. stavo tornando

Page 106, Practice 6

I want to go	I must study	I can bring
we wanted to leave	we had to arrive	we could hear
he/she will want to bring	he/she will have to run	he/she will be able to buy
they wanted to listen	they had to do	they could tell
they wanted to come	they had to go	they could leave

Page 106, Practice 7

voglio pensare	devo andare	posso cantare
volevi scrivere	dovevi vedere	potevi leggere
vorremmo venire	dovremmo comprare	potremmo vendere
hanno voluto giocare	hanno dovuto chiudere	avrebbero potuto pulire

Page 107, Practice 8

1. when was the bill paid?, 2. by whom was the Divine Comedy written? 3. America was discovered in 1492, 4. the boy was woken up, 5. the house is finished

Page 107, Practice 9

1. l'inglese è studiato da molti, 2. la partita è stata giocata sotto la pioggia, 3. quando è stato trovato il cane? 4. la casa è pulita da Paolo, 5. la macchina è stata venduta in fretta

Page 109, Practice 10

Present

1. disdico, 2. rifai, 3. fraintendete, 4. intervengono, 5. tolgo, 6. rifa, 7. suppongono, 8. ottiene, 9. interdicono, 10. rivediamo

Future

1. rifarò, 2. contenderanno, 3. supporrà, 4. prevedremo, 5. rifarete, 6. opporremo, 7. otterranno, 8. predirò, 9. contraddirà, 10. interverranno

Passato Remoto

1. addivennero, 2. previde, 3. soddisfecero, 4. predicemmo, 5. tolsi, 6. fraintendeste, 7. propose, 8. contraddissero, 9. prevenisti, 10. contraffecero

Passato Prossimo

1. ho stupefatto, 2. hai opposto, 3. abbiamo disdetto, 4. hanno previsto, 5. ha ottenuto, 6. hai preteso

Page 110, Practice 11

1. predissero, 2. distenderemo, 3. diviene, 4. perverremo, 5. interdirà, 6. supposero, 7. contraffanno, 8. preveniamo, 9. prevedrà, 10. opponi, 11. soddisfaranno, 12. fraintendete, 13. raccolse, 14. contradici, 15. contendemmo, 16. toglierò, 17. stupefaranno, 18. avvide, 19. rifaccio, 20. distendeste, 21. supponiamo, 22. proposi, 23. distogliamo, 24. raccoglie, 25. disdirò, 26. contraffaremo, 27. opponi, 28. diveniste, 29. togliemmo, 30. intervenne

Chapter 10

Page 111, Practice 1

Io:	parlo	vedo	sento	capisco
Tu:	cammini	scrivi	parti	finisci
Lui:	lavora	legge	viene	pulisce
Lei:	cucina	teme	dice	esce
Noi:	insegniamo	vogliamo	scopriamo	offriamo
Voi:	arrivate	vincete	avvenite	riuscite
Loro:	cambiano	perdono	muoiono	salgono

Page 112, Practice 2

cominciavo, parlavi, arrivava, mangiava
perdeva, vinceva, dicevamo, davano
venivamo, capivi, finiva, salivo
parlavo, diventavi, comprava, passavamo
leggevi, eravamo, scrivevate, dovevano
finivamo, dicevate, capivano, finivi
chiudevo, arrivavi, partiva, usciva
cambiavamo, scrivevate, entravano, fuggivi
avevo, dovevi, andavamo, era
potevamo, facevi, usciva, volevano
venivano, diceva, uscivano, finiva
andavo, capivano, finivate, partivi

Page 113, Practice 3

A. 1. I'll eat, 2. you'll (s.) hear, 3. he'll climb, 4. we'll buy, 5. we'll make/do, 6. I'll study, 7. I'll hear, 8. he/she listens, 9. you'll (pl.) leave, 10. you'll (pl.) understand, 11. I'll make/do, 12. you'll (s.) want, 13. you'll (pl.) have to, 14. you'll (pl.) get up, 15. I'll drive, 16. we'll fly, 17. you'll (s.) stop, 18. I'll know, 19. I'll know, 20. we'll arrive, 21. I'll stay, 22. we'll be, 23. you'll (pl.) read

B. 1. andrò, 2. dormirai, 3. mangerà, 4. pulirò, 5. camminerà, 6. chiamerete, 7. ascolterò, 8. cambierai, 9. staremo, 10. entreranno, 11. riderò, 12. potremo, 13. vedrò, 14. andrete, 15. scriveranno, 16. risponderà, 17. dovrò, 18. dimenticherò, 19. pulirà, 20. staranno, 21. farò, 22. chiuderà, 23. berranno

Page 114, Practice 4

	Passato Remoto	Passato Prossimo
Io:	andai	sono andato/a
Tu:	facesti	hai fatto
Lui:	venne	è venuto
Lei:	capì	ha capito
Noi:	vedemmo	abbiamo visto
Voi:	pensaste	avete pensato
Loro:	sentirono	hanno sentito
Io:	stetti	sono stato/a
Tu:	chiedesti	hai chiesto
Lui:	mandò	ha mandato
Lei:	pensò	ha pensato

Page 115, Practice 5

A. 1. I had eaten, 2. we had understood, 3. they had slept, 4. they had left, 5. I had gone, 6. we had been, 7. we had spoken, 8. you (s.) had studied, 9. I had understood, 10. I had closed, 11. you (s.) had heard, 12. we had brought, 13. he had lost, 14. you (pl.) had won, 15. I had telephoned, 16. she had finished, 17. I had been, 18. they had climbed, 19. she had descended, 20. you (pl.) had left, 21. we had been sorry, 22. they had died, 23. I had entered

B. 1. avevo dormito, 2. era entrato, 3. aveva parlato, 4. avevamo capito, 5. avevate fatto, 6. aveva fatto, 7. aveva scritto, 8. eri stato/a, 9. aveva visto, 10. eravamo venuti/e, 11. erano ritornati/e, 12. eravamo andati/e, 13. avevo mangiato, 14. avevi scritto, 15. avevano pulito, 16. avevamo letto, 17. aveva messo, 18. avevamo detto, 19. avevo saputo, 20. aveva visto, 21. avevo voluto, 22. avevate detto, 23. era nata

Page 116, Practice 6

1. vorrei (mi piacerebbe), 2. leggerei, 3. parlereste, 4. ascolterebbe, 5. pulirei, 6. scriverebbero, 7. penseremmo, 8. risponderei, 9. leggeresti, 10. mangerebbe, 11. venderebbe, 12. studieremmo, 13. scierei, 14. viaggerebbero, 15. berreste, 16. studierei, 17. dovrei, 18. potrei, 19. vorresti, 20. penseremmo, 21. chiuderebbero, 22. apriremmo, 23. capirebbe

Page 117, Practice 7

1. avrei voluto (mi sarebbe piaciuto), 2. sarei stato/a, 3. avrebbe parlato, 4. avrei ascoltato, 5. avreste pulito, 6. avrebbero scritto, 7. avrebbero pensato, 8. avrebbe letto, 9. avremmo mangiato, 10. sarebbero arrivati/e, 11. sarei stato/a, 12. saremmo stati/e, 13. avresti bevuto, 14. avrebbe studiato, 15. sarebbe andata, 16. avreste voluto, 17. avrei chiuso, 18. avrebbe aperto, 19. avrebbe pensato, 20. avremmo capito, 21. avrebbero viaggiato, 22. avresti cantato, 23. avrebbero guardato, 24. saremmo venuti/e

Present Subjunctive	**Imperfect Subjunctive**
1. mangi	mangiassi
2. veda	vedessi
3. parli	parlasse
4. senta	sentisse
5. chiudiamo	chiudessimo
6. capiate	capiste
7. vengano	venissero
8. rispondiamo	rispondessimo
9. scriva	scrivessi
10. impari	imparassi
11. finisca	finisse
12. mangiamo	mangiassimo
13. beviate	beveste
14. sappiano	sapessero
15. telefoni	telefonassi
16. prenda	prendesse
17. stiate	steste
18. stia	stessi
19. dobbiate	doveste
20. capiscano	capissero
21. legga	leggesse
22. mandi	mandassi
23. venda	vendesse

Page 119, Practice 9

1. sia venuto/a	fossi venuto/a
2. abbia parlato	avesse parlato
3. abbiamo ascoltato	avessimo ascoltato
4. abbia fatto	avesse fatto
5. abbiate finito	aveste finito
6. siate andati/e	foste andati/e
7. abbiano chiuso	avessero chiuso
8. abbia aperto	avessi aperto
9. abbia potuto	avessi potuto
10. abbia detto	avesse detto
11. abbiamo finito	avessimo finito
12. abbia capito	avessi capito
13. abbia risposto	avessi risposto
14. abbia visto	avesse visto
15. abbiate parlato	aveste parlato
16. abbia vissuto	avessi vissuto
17. abbia preso	avesse preso
18. abbiano viaggiato	avessero viaggiato
19. abbia ordinato	avessi ordinato
20. abbiate insegnato	aveste insegnato
21. abbia bevuto	avessi bevuto
22. abbia aspettato	avesse aspettato
23. abbia ricevuto	avessi ricevuto

Page 120, Practice 10

	Present	Future	Imperfect	Passato Remoto
Io:	faccio	farò	facevo	feci
Tu:	vai	andrai	andavi	andasti
Lui:	mangia	mangerà	mangiava	mangiò
Lei:	parla	parlerà	parlava	parlò
Noi:	leggiamo	leggeremo	leggevamo	leggemmo
Voi:	bevete	berrete	bevevate	beveste
Loro:	vedono	vedranno	vedevano	videro
Io:	sento	sentirò	sentivo	sentii
Lui:	dà	darà	dava	diede
Voi:	state	starete	stavate	steste
Lei:	capisce	capirà	capiva	capì
Loro:	finiscono	finiranno	finivano	finirono
Io:	rispondo	risponderò	rispondevo	risposi
Lui:	pulisce	pulirà	puliva	pulì
Noi:	arriviamo	arriveremo	arrivavamo	arrivammo
Voi:	salite	salirete	salivate	saliste
Tu:	soffri	soffrirai	soffrivi	soffristi
Lei:	offre	offirà	offriva	offrì
Io:	imparo	imparerò	imparavo	imparai
Loro:	vede	vedrà	vedeva	vide
Lei:	cade	cadrà	cadeva	cadde
Lui:	muore	morirà	moriva	morì

Page 121, Practice 11

1. ho capito — avevo capito
2. hai visto — avevi visto
3. ha finito — aveva finito
4. ha letto — aveva letto
5. siamo ritornati/e — eravamo ritornati/e
6. avete imparato — avevate imparato
7. hanno cenato — avevano cenato
8. ho pranzato — avevo pranzato
9. ha venduto — aveva venduto
10. ha acceso — aveva acceso
11. avete accettato — avevate accettato
12. hanno spento — avevano spento
13. ho lavato — avevo lavato
14. siamo usciti/e — eravamo usciti/e
15. hai viaggiato — avevi viaggiato
16. è partito — era partito
17. ha guarito — aveva guarito
18. siete arrivati/e — eravate arrivati/e
19. hai ascoltato — avevi ascoltato
20. hanno saltato — avevano saltato
21. ha esaminato — aveva esaminato
22. abbiamo diviso — avevamo diviso
23. ha stirato — aveva stirato

Page 122, Practice 12

1.	parlerei	avrei parlato
2.	arriveresti	saresti arrivato/a
3.	canterebbe	avrebbe cantato
4.	laverebbe	avrebbe lavato
5.	lavorerebbe	avrebbe lavorato
6.	staremmo	saremmo stati/e
7.	andreste	sareste andati/e
8.	viaggerebbero	avrebbero viaggiato
9.	vedrei	avrei visto
10.	potresti	avresti potuto
11.	leggerebbe	avrebbe letto
12.	scriverebbe	avrebbe scritto
13.	correremmo	saremmo corsi/e
14.	rispondereste	avreste risposto
15.	cadrebbero	sarebbero caduti/e
16.	capirei	avrei capito
17.	finiresti	avresti finito
18.	verrebbe	sarebbe venuto
19.	sentiremmo	avremmo sentito
20.	offrireste	avreste offerto
21.	pulirebbero	avrebbero pulito

Page 123, Practice 13

	Present	Imperfect	Past	Pluperfect Subjunctive
Io:	vada	andassi	sia andato/a	fossi andato/a
Tu:	ritorni	ritornassi	sia ritornato/a	fossi ritornato/a
Lui:	dia	desse	abbia dato	avesse dato
Lei:	faccia	facesse	abbia fatto	avesse fatto
Noi:	stiamo	stessimo	siamo stati/e	fossimo stati/e
Voi:	beviate	beveste	abbiate bevuto	aveste bevuto
Loro:	vedano	vedessero	abbiano visto	avessero visto
Noi:	fermiamo	fermassimo	abbiamo fermato	avessimo fermato
Lui:	senta	sentisse	abbia sentito	avesse sentito
Lei:	divida	dividesse	abbia diviso	avesse diviso
Lui:	paghi	pagasse	abbia pagato	avesse pagato
Tu:	venda	vendessi	abbia venduto	avessi venduto
Io:	dorma	dormissi	abbia dormito	avessi dormito
Loro:	contino	contassero	abbiano contato	avessero contato
Voi:	diciate	diceste	abbiate detto	aveste detto
Lei:	giochi	giocasse	abbia giocato	avesse giocato
Lui:	salti	saltasse	abbia saltato	avesse saltato
Noi:	guardiamo	guardassimo	abbiamo guardato	avessimo guardato
Tu:	salga	salissi	sia salito/a	fossi salito/a
Voi:	leggiate	leggeste	abbiate letto	aveste letto
Loro:	tirino	tirassero	abbiano tirato	avessero tirato
Noi:	pensiamo	pensassimo	abbiamo pensato	avessimo pensato

Chapter 11

Page 125, Practice 2

1. ho bisogno di scarpe, 2. ho caldo, 3. hai freddo, 4. abbiamo fretta, 5. hammo mal di testa, 6. ho paura, 7. ha sete, 8. aveva sonno, 9. avevano ragione, 10. avevo torto, 11. abbiamo vergogna, 12. ho voglia di mangiare, 13. avevate fame, 14. avevano fretta, 15. avrei sete, 16. avrebbero bisogno di scarpe, 17. avrebbe ragione, 18. avremmo torto, 19. avrei paura, 20. avrebbe intenzione, 21. ho avuto mal di testa, 22. hanno avuto paura, 23. abbiamo avuto paura

Page 128, Practice 4

1. facciamo alla romana, 2. fa attenzione, 3. faccio calazione, 4. facciamo un bagno, 5. hanno fatto una crociera, 6. fa la spesa, 7. ti sei fatto/a male, 8. faccio un favore, 9. fanno una passeggiata, 10. farò fotografie, 11. ha fatto un viaggio, 12. fate una domanda, 13. fa uno spuntino, 14. facciamo in fretta, 15. fa caldo, 16. facciamo un regalo, 17. facciamo una visita, 18. faceva freddo, 19. fa la predica, 20. farà un discorso, 21. fanno quattro chicciere, 22. ha fatto brutta figura

Page 133, Practice 10

1. We learn to ski, 2. I start to understand, 3. I forgot to study, 4. I'm thinking of coming, 5. he/she needs to study, 6. he/she thought about you, 7. we'll stay home, 8. they'll return to Rome, 9. I am afraid of everything, 10. they wait to come, 11. I need you, 12. she continues to eat, 13. he/she used to teach driving, 14. you (pl.) hope you see, 15. I realize I'm late, 16. he/she falls in love with everybody, 17. I don't trust him, 18. she lives on love, 19. stop (s.) talking, 20. you count (pl.) on your sister, 21. he/she tried walking, 22. he/she pretends to look in the book, 23. we laugh at him, 24. they give thanks for everything

Page 134, Practice 11

1. vado a ballare, 2. andiamo a studiare, 3. sei stato/a a Roma?, 4. credo nei fantasmi, 5. pensano alle vacanze, 6. proverò a venire, 7. pensiamo di andare, 8. ti insegnerò a nuotare, 9. finisco de lavorare, 10. ha voglia de mangiare cioccolata, 11. comincio a parlare, 12. si ferma a Parigi, 13. cerchiamo di venire, 14. chiamami prima de partire, 15. continui a studiare, 16. hanno promesso di andare, 17. ho promesso di venire, 18. hanno bisogno di pensare, 19. sperate di dormire, 20. hanno voglia de viaggiare, 21. smetti di parlare, 22. fanno attenzione all'insegnante

Chapter 12

Page 135, *-are* Verbs

abitare
1. Dove abiti? Abito a Napoli. 2. Abitano in Italia da molto tempo. 3. Quando ero giovane, abitavo in Florida. 4. Vorrebbe abitare in una casa grande. 5. Spera di abitare vicino al mare.

addormentare
6. Questo film mi fa addormentare. 7. La donna si è addormentata sul divano. 8. Questa lezione mi fa addormentare. 9. Io mi addormento con la luce accesa.

addormentarsi
10. Paolo si addormenta davanti alla televisione. 11. Non addormentarti al cinema. 12. Il bambino si è addormentato subito.

alzare (qualche cosa)
13. Per favore, alza il riscaldamento. 14. Dovrebbe alzare la voce, nessuno lo sente.

alzarsi
15. Il giovane si alza sempre tardi. 16. In inverno, il sole si alza tardi.

andare
17. Vanno a scuola alle otto. 18. Dove sei andato ieri sera? 19. Vorrei che lei andasse all'università. 20. È andata a Roma con me. 21. A marzo andremo in Italia.

andare a
22. Non vado a scuola questa sera. 23. Vorresti andare a ballare? 24. Il prossimo mese andrò a visitare degli amici. 25. Potresti andare all'ufficio postale? 26. La prossima settimana andrò al museo. 27. Lei vorrebbe andare a sciare con noi.

andare da + article

28. È andata dal dottore. 29. Vorrei andare dal macellaio. 30. Penso che siano andati dal loro amico.

andare in

31. Il prossimo anno vorrei andare in Italia. 32. Andrà in Cina con degli amici. 33. Andranno in macchina o in aereo? 34. Mia mamma è andata in cucina.

arrivare

35. I miei amici arriveranno domani. 36. Il tuo biglietto è arrivato ieri. 37. Spero (che) siano arrivati bene.

arrivare a

38. Sono arrivati all'aereoporto. 39. Arriverò a Venezia fra una settimana.

arrivare in

40. Sono arrivati in America con la nave. 41. Ha detto che è arrivata in Cina. 42. Vorrei arrivare in Grecia in estate. 43. Arriverò domani in macchina.

arrivare in

44. Siamo arrivati negli Stati Uniti. 45. I turisti arrivano in estate.

aspettare

46. Aspetto mia sorella. 47. L'ho aspettato per tanto tempo.

chiamare

48. Hanno chiamato un tassi un'ora fa. 49. Sta molto male, dobbiamo chiamare il dottore. 50. Vogliono chiamarla, ma è troppo tardi.

chiamarsi

51. Non so come ti chiami. 52. Come si chiama tua sorella? Si chiama Carla.

dare

53. Gli ho dato un libro. 54. Sperava (che) gli dessero il primo premio. 55. Potresti darmi la tua macchina sabato? 56. Il presidente ha dato le dimissioni. 57. Mi ha dato tanti soldi.

desiderare

58. Il bambino desidera molti regali per Natale. 59. Carlo desidera parlarti. 60. Desideri vedere qualche cosa? 61. Al ristorante desiderava provare tutto. 62. Desideri una tazza di caffè o (di) tè? 63. Desideriamo che tu venga a visitarci.

diventare

64. Carla è diventata alta. 65. Verdi è diventato molto famoso. 66. La gente in Italia sta diventando molto vecchia. 67. È diventata una bella ragazza.

fare

68. Che cosa mi suggerisci di fare? 69. Tutti i giorni lei fa i biscotti. 70. Ha fatto un bel vestito. 71. Vorrei fare la maestra. 72. Ieri faceva molto freddo. 73. In estate fa molto caldo. 74. Spero (che) farai una bella vacanza. 75. Stanno facendo una strada nuova. 76. Sperava di fare una lunga passeggiata. 77. L'artista ha fatto una bella statua.

guardare

78. L'insegnante lo guarda. 79. Hai guardato il suo compito? 80. Mi guardava fisso.

mandare

81. Manda a letto i bambini. 82. Ha mandato a letto i bambini. 83. Manderò il pacco per posta. 84. Speravo (che) tu mi mandassi il tuo libro. 85. Devi mandare il libro per posta. 86. Ti mando un bacio.

pensare

87. Penso (che) sia troppo freddo per uscire. 88. Pensa chi ho visto ieri sera? 89. Avrebbero dovuto pensarci.

sognare

90. Ho sognato che volavo. 91. Giovanna sognava ad occhi aperti. 92. Non avrei mai sognato di vincere la lotteria.

stare

93. I bambini vogliono stare dentro oggi. 94. Starò in Italia per due settimane. 95. Bambini, state zitti! 96. Mia madre stava alla finestra. 97. I miei amici stanno a Roma.

Page 140, *-ere* Verbs

accendere

1. Accendi la luce, per piacere. 2. Non voglio che tu accenda la sigaretta.

avere

3. Suo figlio ha l'influenza. 4. I loro parenti non hanno soldi per vivere. 5. L'avrei fatto, se avessi avuto tempo. 6. Avevano molti amici. 7. Hai fame? Sì, ho molta fame. 8. Quel bambino ha molta fortuna. 9. La mia amica ha sempre fretta. 10. La donna aveva un bel vestito.

bere

11. Quell'uomo beve troppo. 12. Beviamo alla nostra salute. 13. Penso (che) gli piaccia bere vino rosso.

chiedere

14. Mi ha chiesto aiuto. 15. Mia madre chiede sempre di te. 16. Quanto chiedi per questa casa?

chiudere

17. I negozi chiudono alle 7:30. 18. Non chiudi mai la porta. 19. Hai chiuso la bottiglia? 20. L'ho chiuso fuori di casa.

conoscere

21. Tuo padre conosce bene l'Italia. 22. Conosci un bravo dottore? 23. Ho conosciuto mio marito in Africa. 24. Non la conosco bene.

correre

25. Quel bambino correva come il vento. 26. Il treno corre velocemente. 27. Dobbiamo correre per prendere l'autobus. 28. I bambini non possono correre in piscina.

credere a, in

29. Nessuno lo crede. 30. Paolo non crede in Dio.

credere che

31. Non credevo (che) fossero già arrivati. 32. Crede che domani pioverà.

decidere di

33. Non posso decidere quando andare in Italia. 34. Ha deciso di rispettare le regole della scuola. 35. Decideranno presto dove andare in vacanza.

difendere

36. Lei difende sempre suo fratello. 37. I soldati hanno difeso la città dai nemici. 38. I guanti difendono le mani dal freddo.

dispiacere

39. Ti dispiacerebbe se venissi a casa con te? 40. Mi dispiace non poterti visitare. 41. Se non ti dispiace, vorrei riposare. 42. Mi dispiace che tua mamma non sia potuta venire.

dovere

43. Che cosa dovrei fare? 44. Non dovrei dirti questa storia. 45. Carlo è diventato un grande scrittore. 46. Non devi comprarlo oggi.

essere

47. Di dove sei? Sei americano? 48. Che ore sono? È presto o è tardi? 49. Paolo non è in casa. 50. Che sarà, sarà. 51. Non è possibile che vengano. 52. Non era possibile che venissero. 53. Che cosa è successo?

mettere

54. Mettiamo tutti i libri sulla scrivania. 55. Abbiamo messo le tende sulle finestre. 56. Hai messo via le valige?

mettersi

57. Si è messa il suo nuovo costume da bagno. 58. Si è messa a piangere. 59. Si è messo vicino alla finestra.

nascere

60. Mio figlio è nato il 12 ottobre. 61. Credi che io sia nata ieri? 62. Tua sorella è nata a Venezia. 63. Il sole si alza a est. 64. Nascono come i funghi.

rispondere

65. Spero che tu risponderai alla mia lettera. 66. Perchè non hai risposto? 67. Nessuno risponde al telefono.

rispondere di

68. I bambini devono rispondere del vetro rotto. 69. Lei deve rispondere delle sue azioni.

scrivere

70. Come si scrive il tuo cognome? 71. Devo scrivere a macchina la lettera? 72. Lei ha scritto al consolato italiano. 73. Dante ha scritto molto nella sua vita. 74. Lei spera che le scriverai presto. 75. Gli ho scritto di non venire.

tenere

76. Il bambino teneva in mano un giocattolo. 77. La polizia teneva in dietro la gente. 78. Ho tenuto l'acqua nel frigorifero. 79. Posso tenere il cappotto? Ho freddo. 80. Lei vuole tenere le finestre chiuse.

vedere

81. Hai visto un bel film? 82. Vorrei vederlo felice. 83. Non vedo l'ora di partire per l'Italia. 84. Si vede ancora la macchia? 85. Abbiamo visto una stella cadente. 86. Lui andrà a vedere sua mamma. 87. Loro andavano a vederlo sciare.

vendere

88. Lui vende libri. 89. Lei ha venduto molte case. 90. Loro vendono all'ingrosso. 91. Non mi piace vendere.

volere

92. Loro vorrebbero viaggiare, ma non possono. 93. Oggi, la mia macchina non vuole funzionare. 94. Lei non vuole che tu venga domani. 95. Vorrei (che) tu glielo dicessi. 96. Lei vuole studiare l'italiano. 97. Vogliamo vedere i tuoi quadri. 98. Lui vuole comprare una macchina nuova.

Page 145, -ire Verbs

aprire

1. Apri la porta, per favore. 2. Vuole aprire un conto corrente. 3. Non aprire la televisione. 4. La banda apriva la parata.

aprirsi

5. I fiori primaverili si sono aperti. 6. La finestra dell'appartamento si apre sul mare. 7. La scuola si apre in autunno.

costruire

8. Stanno costruendo una nuova autostrada. 9. Spero di costruire una casa nuova. 10. Con molto lavoro, ti puoi costruire una fortuna.

dire

11. I bambini dicono spesso le bugie. 12. Suo padre glielo aveva detto. 13. Lei gli ha detto di chiamarci quando arrivano. 14. Spero (che) tu non abbia detto niente. 15. Digli la verità. 16. Il testimone ha detto che non aveva visto l'incidente.

divertire

17. I cartoni animati divertono i bambini. 18. La donna si diverte con i bambini.

divertirsi

19. Ti sei divertito a New York? 20. Divertiti! 21. Il bambino si diverte a giocare con i Legos. 22. Io al circo non mi diverto.

finire

23. Io so già come finisce il libro. 24. La lezione finisce alle 9:00 di sera. 25. Hai finito? 26. Hai finito tutti i soldi? 27. Il gelato è finito. 28. Non ho finito i miei compiti.

partire

29. Sono partiti per l'Italia in aereo. 30. I miei amici sono partiti ieri per la spiaggia. 31. Il treno parte alle 10:00 esatte. 32. Io partirò martedì. 33. Sono partiti presto.

preferire

34. Mia madre preferisce il caffè al tè. 35. Io preferisco più leggere che guardare la televisione. 36. Preferisco che tu stia dentro. 37. Preferiscono più sciare che pattinare.

pulire

38. Ogni venerdì io pulisco la casa. 39. Pulisci le scarpe prima di entrare. 40. Pulisciti il naso.

salire

41. La nave spaziale saliva molto velocemente. 42. Devi salire al terzo piano. 43. Il prezzo della frutta è salito ancora. 44. Deve salire sull'autobus. 45. Mia figlia è salita con l'ascensore.

sentire

46. La madre ha sentito il bambino piangere. 47. Hai sentito il concerto? 48. Vorrei sentire la tua opinione. 49. Mio nonno non sente bene.

soffrire

50. Giovanna soffre di mal di testa. 51. Soffrono di fame. 52. Gli alberi di arancio hanno sofferto per il gelo.

spedire

53. Ti spedirò una lettera. 54. Ti hanno spedito una scatola grande. 55. Vorrei spedirti un regalo.

uscire

56. Tuo padre è uscito a piedi. 57. I miei amici sono usciti mezz'ora fa. 58. Non uscire, piove.

venire

59. Vorresti venire con noi? 60. Sono venuti in Italia tanti anni fa. 61. Penso (che) stia venendo qualcuno. 62. A che ora sei venuto a casa? 63. Da dove viene quella ragazza? 64. Questo olio viene dalla fattoria. 65. La neve veniva giù lentamente.

Verb Charts

Regular Verbs

Verbs Ending in *-are*

Parlare

Present Indicative
parlo, parli, parla, parliamo,
parlate, parlano

Imperfect
parlavo, parlavi, parlava,
parlavamo, parlavate, parlavano

Future
parlerò, parlerai, parlerà,
parleremo, parlerete, parleranno

Imperative
parla, parliamo, parlate
parli (pol. s.), parlino (pol pl.)

Passato Remoto (Preterite)
parlai, parlasti, parlò,
parlammo, parlaste, parlarono

Passato Prossimo (Present Perfect)
ho parlato, hai parlato, ha parlato,
abbiamo parlato, avete parlato,
hanno parlato

Verbs Ending in *-ere*

Perdere

perdo, perdi, perde, perdiamo,
perdete, perdono

perdevo, perdevi, perdeva,
perdevamo, perdevate, perdevano

perderò, perderai, perderà,
perderemo, perderete, perderanno

perdi, perdiamo, perdete
perda (pol. s.), perdano (pol. pl.)

perdei, perdesti, perdè,
perdemmo, perdeste, perderono

ho perduto, hai perduto, ha perduto,
abbiamo perduto, avete perduto,
hanno perduto

Parlare

Trapassato Prossimo (Pluperfect)
avevo parlato, avevi parlato,
aveva parlato, avevamo parlato,
avevate parlato, avevano parlato

Present Conditional
parlerei, parleresti, parlerebbe,
parleremmo, parlereste, parlerebbero

Past Conditional
avrei parlato, avresti parlato,
avrebbe parlato, avremmo parlato,
avreste parlato, avrebbero parlato

Present Subjunctive
che io parli, tu parli, lui/lei parli,
noi parliamo, voi parliate,
loro parlino

Imperfect Subjunctive
che io parlassi, tu parlassi,
lui/lei parlasse, noi parlassimo,
voi parlaste, loro parlassero

Past Subjunctive
che io abbia parlato, tu abbia
parlato, lui/lei abbia parlato,
noi abbiamo parlato, voi abbiate
parlato, loro abbiano parlato

Pluperfect Subjunctive
che io avessi parlato, tu avessi
parlato, lui/lei avesse parlato,
noi avessimo parlato, voi aveste
parlato, loro avessero parlato

Perdere

avevo perduto, avevi perduto,
aveva perduto, avevamo perduto,
avevate perduto, avevano perduto

perderei, perderesti, perderebbe,
perderemmo, perdereste, perderebbero

avrei perduto, avresti perduto,
avrebbe perduto, avremmo perduto,
avreste perduto, avrebbero perduto

che io perda, tu perda, lui/lei perda,
noi perdiamo, voi perdiate,
loro perdano

che io perdessi, tu perdessi,
lui/lei perdesse, noi perdessimo,
voi perdeste, loro perdessero

che io abbia perduto, tu abbia
perduto, lui/lei abbia perduto,
noi abbiamo perduto, voi abbiate
perduto, loro abbiano perduto

che io avessi perduto, tu avessi
perduto, lui/lei avesse perduto,
noi avessimo perduto, voi aveste
perduto, loro avessero perduto

Verbs Ending in -ire

Dormire

Present Indicative
dormo, dormi, dorme, dormiamo,
dormite, dormono

Imperfect
dormivo, dormivi, dormiva
dormivamo, dormivate, dormivano

Future
dormirò, dormirai, dormirà,
dormiremo, dormirete, dormiranno

Imperative
dormi, dormiamo, dormite
dorma (pol. s), dormano (pol. pl.)

Passato Remoto (Preterite)
dormii, dormisti, dormì, dormimmo,
dormiste, dormirono

Passato Prossimo (Present Perfect)
ho dormito, hai dormito, ha dormito,
abbiamo dormito, avete dormito,
hanno dormito

Trapassato Prossimo (Pluperfect)
avevo dormito, avevi dormito,
aveva dormito, avevamo dormito,
avevate dormito, avevano dormito

Verbs Ending in -ire (with isc)

Finire

finisco, finisci, finisce, finiamo,
finite, finiscono

finivo, finivi, finiva,
finivamo, finivate, finivano

finirò, finirai, finirà,
finiremo, finirete, finiranno

finisci, finiamo, finite
finisca (pol. s.), finiscano (pol. pl.)

finii, finisti, finì, finimmo,
finiste, finirono

ho finito, hai finito, ha finito,
abbiamo finito, avete finito,
hanno finito

avevo finito, avevi finito,
aveva finito, avevamo finito,
avevate finito, avevano finito

Dormire

Present Conditional
dormirei, dormiresti, dormirebbe,
dormiremmo, dormireste, dormirebbero

Past Conditional
avrei dormito, avresti dormito,
avrebbe dormito, avremmo dormito,
avreste dormito, avrebbero dormito

Present Subjunctive
che io dorma, tu dorma, lui/lei dorma,
noi dormiamo, voi dormiate,
loro dormano

Imperfect Subjunctive
che io dormissi, tu dormissi,
lui/lei dormisse, noi dormissimo,
voi dormiste, loro dormissero

Past Subjunctive
che io abbia dormito, tu abbia
dormito, lui/lei abbia dormito,
noi abbiamo dormito, voi abbiate
dormito, loro abbiano dormito

Pluperfect Subjunctive
che io avessi dormito, tu avessi
dormito, lui/lei avesse dormito,
noi avessimo dormito, voi aveste
dormito, loro avessero dormito

Finire

finirei, finiresti, finirebbe,
finiremmo, finireste, finirebbero

avrei finito, avresti finito,
avrebbe finito, avremmo finito,
avreste finito, avrebbero finito

che io finisca, tu finisca, lui/lei finisca,
noi finiamo, voi finiate,
loro finiscano

che io finissi, tu finissi,
lui/lei finisse, noi finissimo,
voi finiste, loro finissero

che io abbia finito, tu abbia
finito, lui/lei abbia finito,
noi abbiamo finito, voi abbiate
finito, loro abbiano finito

che io avessi finito, tu avessi
finito, lui/lei avesse finito,
noi avessimo finito, voi aveste
finito, loro avessero finito

Common Irregular Verbs

Fare

Dare

Present Indicative
faccio, fai, fa, facciamo,
fate, fanno

do, dai, dà, diamo, date, danno

Imperfect
facevo, facevi, faceva,
facevamo, facevate, facevano

davo, davi, dava, davamo,
davate, davano

Future
farò, farai, farà, faremo,
farete, faranno

darò, darai, darà, daremo,
darete, daranno

Imperative
fà (non fare), facciamo, fate
faccia (pol. s.), facciano (pol. pl.)

dà (non dare), diamo, date
dia (pol. s.), diano (pol. pl.)

Passato Remoto (Preterite)
feci, facesti, fece, facemmo,
faceste, facero

diedi, desti, diede, demmo,
deste, diedero

Passato Prossimo (Present Perfect)
ho fatto, hai fatto, ha fatto,
abbiamo fatto, avete fatto,
hanno fatto

ho dato, hai dato, ha dato,
abbiamo dato, avete dato,
hanno dato

Trapassato Prossimo (Pluperfect)
avevo fatto, avevi fatto,
aveva fatto, avevamo fatto,
avevate fatto, avevano fatto

avevo dato, avevi dato,
aveva dato, avevamo dato,
avevate dato, avevano dato

Fare	Dare

Fare

Present Conditional
farei, faresti, farebbe,
faremmo, fareste, farebbero

Past Conditional
avrei fatto, avresti fatto,
avrebbe fatto, avremmo fatto,
avreste fatto, avrebbero fatto

Present Subjunctive
che io faccia, tu faccia, lui/lei faccia,
noi facciamo, voi facciate,
loro facciano

Imperfect Subjunctive
che io facessi, tu facessi,
lui/lei facesse, noi facessimo,
voi faceste, loro facessero

Past Subjunctive
che io abbia fatto, tu abbia
fatto, lui/lei abbia fatto,
noi abbiamo fatto, voi abbiate
fatto, loro abbiano fatto

Pluperfect Subjunctive
che io avessi fatto, tu avessi
fatto, lui/lei avesse fatto,
noi avessimo fatto, voi aveste
fatto, loro avessero fatto

Dare

Present Conditional
darei, daresti, darebbe,
daremmo, dareste, darebbero

Past Conditional
avrei dato, avresti dato,
avrebbe dato, avremmo dato,
avreste dato, avrebbero dato

Present Subjunctive
che io dia, tu dia, lui/lei dia,
noi diamo, voi diate,
loro diano

Imperfect Subjunctive
che io dessi, tu dessi,
lui/lei desse, noi dessimo,
voi deste, loro dessero

Past Subjunctive
che io abbia dato, tu abbia
dato, lui/lei abbia dato,
noi abbiamo dato, voi abbiate
dato, loro abbiano dato

Pluperfect Subjunctive
che io avessi dato, tu avessi
dato, lui/lei avesse dato,
noi avessimo dato, voi aveste
dato, loro avessero dato

Vedere

Present Indicative
vedo, vedi, vede, vediamo,
vedete, vedono

Imperfect
vedevo, vedevi, vedeva,
vedevamo, vedevate, vedevano

Future
vedrò, vedrai, vedrà, vedremo,
vedrete, vedranno

Imperative
vedi (non vedere), vediamo, vedete
veda (pol. s.), vedano (pol. pl.)

Passato Remoto (Preterite)
vidi, vedesti, vide, vedemmo,
vedeste, videro

Passato Prossimo (Present Perfect)
ho visto, hai visto, ha visto,
abbiamo visto, avete visto,
hanno visto

Trapassato Prossimo (Pluperfect)
avevo visto, avevi visto,
aveva visto, avevamo visto,
avevate visto, avevano visto

Venire

vengo, vieni, viene, veniamo,
venite, vengono

venivo, venivi, veniva, venivamo,
venivate, venivano

verrò, verrai, verrà, verremo,
verrete, verranno

vieni (non venire), veniamo, venite
venga (pol. s.), vengano (pol. pl.)

venni, venisti, venne, venimmo,
veniste, vennero

sono venuto/a, sei venuto/a,
lui/lei è venuto/a, noi siamo venuti/e,
voi siete venuti/e, loro sono venuti/e

ero venuto/a, eri venuto/a,
era venuto/a, eravamo venuti/e,
eravate venuti/e, erano venuti/e

Vedere

Present Conditional
vedrei, vedresti, vedrebbe,
vedremmo, vedreste, vedrebbero

Past Conditional
avrei visto, avresti visto,
avrebbe visto, avremmo visto,
avreste visto, avrebbero visto

Present Subjunctive
che io veda, tu veda, lui/lei veda,
noi vediamo, voi vediate,
loro vedano

Imperfect Subjunctive
che io vedessi, tu vedessi,
lui/lei vedesse, noi vedessimo,
voi vedeste, loro vedessero

Past Subjunctive
che io abbia visto, tu abbia
visto, lui/lei abbia visto,
noi abbiamo visto, voi abbiate
visto, loro abbiano visto

Pluperfect Subjunctive
che io avessi visto, tu avessi
visto, lui/lei avesse visto,
noi avessimo visto, voi aveste
visto, loro avessero visto

Venire

Present Conditional
verrei, verresti, verrebbe,
verremmo, verreste, verrebbero

Past Conditional
sarei venuto/a, saresti venuto/a,
sarebbe venuto/a, saremmo venuti/e,
sareste venuti/e, sarebbero venuti/e

Present Subjunctive
che io venga, tu venga, lui/lei venga,
noi veniamo, voi veniate,
loro vengano

Imperfect Subjunctive
che io venissi, tu venissi,
lui/lei venisse, noi venissimo,
voi veniste, loro venissero

Past Subjunctive
che io sia venuto/a, tu sia
venuto/a, lui/lei sia venuto/a,
noi siamo venuti/e, voi siate
venuti/e, loro siano venuti/e

Pluperfect Subjunctive
che io fossi venuto/a, tu fossi venuto/a,
lui/lei fosse venuto/a,
noi fossimo venuti/e, voi foste venuti/e,
loro fossero venuti/e

Index of Verbs

Italian–English

A

abitare   to live
accadere   to happen
accedere   to access
accendere   to light
accettare   to accept
acconsentire   to agree
aderire   to adhere
aggiungere   to add
aiutare   to help
alzarsi   to get up
amare   to love
andare   to go
apparire   to appear
appendere   to hang
applaudire   to applaud
apprendere   to learn
aprire   to open
arrestare   to arrest
arrivare   to arrive
ascoltare   to listen
aspettare   to wait
assentire   to consent
assistere   to assist
assolvere   to absolve
assumere   to assume, hire
attendere   to attend
attribuire   to attribute
avere   to have
avvenire   to happen
avvertire   to announce

B

ballare   to dance
bere   to drink
benedire   to bless
bollire   to boil

C

cadere   to fall
cambiare   to change
camminare   to walk
cantare   to sing
capire   to understand
cenare   to have supper
chiedere   to ask
chiudere   to close
cogliere   to gather
colpire   to hit
cominciare   to start
comprare   to buy
comprendere   to comprehend
concludere   to conclude
condividere   to share
confondere   to confuse
conoscere   to know
consentire   to agree
conseguire   to result
consistere   to consist
contare   to count
controllare   to control
convertire   to convert
convincere   to convince
coprire   to cover
correggere   to correct
correre   to run
costruire   to build
credere   to believe
crescere   to grow
cucire   to sew
cuocere   to cook

D

dare   to give
decidere   to decide
desiderare   to wish
difendere   to defend
digerire   to digest
dimagrire   to lose weight

dimenticare to forget
dire to tell, say
dirigere to direct
discutere to discuss
distinguere to distinguish
diventare to become
divertire to enjoy
dividere to divide
domandare to ask
donare to donate
dormire to sleep
dovere must

E

eleggere to elect
entrare to enter
esaminare to examine
esaurire to exhaust
esibire to exhibit
esistere to exist
esprimere to express
essere to be

F

fallire to fail
fare to do, make
fermare to stop
ferire to wound
finire to finish
firmare to sign
fuggire to escape

G

garantire to guarantee
gestire to manage
giocare to play
girare to turn
godere to enjoy
guardare to look
guarire to heal
guidare to drive
gustare to taste

I

illustrare to illustrate
imparare to learn
includere to include
inghiottire to swallow
insegnare to teach
inseguire to follow, chase
insistere to insist
interrompere to interrupt
investire to invest
ispezionare to inspect
istruire to instruct
invadere to invade
invitare to invite

L

lasciare to leave
lavare to wash
lavorare to work
leggere to read
litigare to quarrel

M

mandare to send
mangiare to eat
mentire to lie
mettere to put
morire to die
mostrare to show
muovere to move

N

nascere to be born
nascondere to hide
nevicare to snow
notare to notice
nuotare to swim

O

offrire to offer
organizzare to organize

P

pagare to pay
parlare to speak, talk

partire   to leave, depart
pensare   to think
perdere   to lose
perdonare   to forgive
permettere   to allow
piangere   to cry
piantare   to plant
piovere   to rain
porre   to put
portare   to bring
potere   to be able
pranzare   to dine
preferire   to prefer
prendere   to take
pretendere   to pretend
prevenire   to prevent
promettere   to promise
promuovere   to promote
proporre   to propose
proteggere   to protect
provare   to try
provvedere   to provide
pulire   to clean
punire   to punish

R

raccontare   to narrate
raggiungere   to reach
rallentare   to slow down
regalare   to give a gift, donate
restare   to stay
restituire   to return
ricevere   to receive
richiedere   to request
ricordare   to remember
ridere   to laugh
ridurre   to reduce
rimanere   to remain
rimuovere   to remove
riposare   to rest
risolvere   to resolve
rispondere   to answer
ritornare   to return
riunire   to reunite
rompere   to break

S

salire   to climb
saltare   to jump
sapere   to know
scegliere   to choose
scendere   to descend
sciare   to ski
scomparire   to disappear
scoprire   to discover
scrivere   to write
seguire   to follow
sentire   to hear
seppellire   to bury
servire   to serve
soffrire   to suffer
sognare   to dream
sorridere   to smile
sostituire   to substitute
spedire   to send
spegnere   to turn off
spendere   to spend
sperare   to hope
spiegare   to explain
spingere   to push
stabilire   to establish
stare   to stay
stirare   to iron
studiare   to study
succedere   to happen
suggerire   to suggest
suonare   to play
svegliare   to wake up
svenire   to faint

T

tagliare   to cut
telefonare   to telephone
temere   to fear
tenere   to keep
togliere   to remove
tornare   to return
tradire   to betray
tradurre   to translate
trasferire   to transfer
trasmettere   to broadcast
trovare   to find

U

ubbidire to obey
udire to hear
unire to unite
urlare to scream
uscire to go out

V

valere to be worth
vedere to see

vendere to sell
venire to come
vestire to dress
viaggiare to travel
vincere to win
visitare to visit
vivere to live
volare to fly
volere to want
votare to vote

Index of Verbs

English–Italian

A

absolve **assolvere**
accept **accettare**
access **accedere**
add **aggiungere**
adhere **aderire**
agree **acconsentire**
answer **rispondere**
appear **apparire**
applaud **applaudire**
arrest **arrestare**
arrive **arrivare**
ask **chiedere**
assist **assistere**
assume **assumere**
attend **attendere**
attribute **attribuire**

B

be **essere**
be born **nascere**
become **diventare, divenire**
believe **credere**
betray **tradire**
bless **benedire**
blow up **gonfiare**
boil **bollire**
break **rompere**
bring **portare**
build **costruire**
bury **seppellire**
buy **comprare**

C

call **chiamare**
can **potere**
cancel **cancellare**
change **cambiare**
choose **scegliere**
clean **pulire**
climb **salire**
close **chiudere**
come **venire**
complete **completare**
comprehend **comprendere**
conclude **concludere**
confuse **confondere**
consent **consentire**
control **controllare**
convert **convertire**
convince **convincere**
cook **cuocere**
correct **correggere**
count **contare**
cover **coprire**
cry **piangere**
cut **tagliare**

D

dance **ballare**
decide **decidere**
defend **difendere**
define **definire**
depart **partire**
descend **scendere**
die **morire**
digest **digerire**
dine **cenare**
direct **dirigere**
disappear **sparire**
discover **scoprire**
discuss **discutere**
distinguish **distinguere**
divide **dividere**
do **fare**
donate **donare**
dream **sognare**
dress **vestire**
drink **bere**

E

eat **mangiare**
elect **eleggere**
enjoy **godere**
enter **entrare**
escape **fuggire**
establish **stabilire**
examine **esaminare**
exhaust **esaurire**
exhibit **esibire**
exist **esistere**
expire **scadere**
explain **spiegare**
express **esprimere**

F

fail **fallire**
fall **cadere**
fear **temere**
feed **nutrire**
find **trovare**
finish **finire**
flee **scappare**
fly **volare**
follow **seguire**
forget **dimenticare**
forgive **perdonare**

G

gather **raccogliere**
get up **alzarsi**
give up **arrendersi**
give **dare**
give a gift **regalare**
go **andare**
go crazy **impazzire**
go out **uscire**
grow **crescere**
guarantee **garantire**

H

hang **appendere**
happen **accadere**
have **avere**
heal **guarire**

hear **sentire, udire**
help **aiutare**
hide **nascondere**
hope **sperare**

I

illustrate **illustrare**
include **includere**
insert **inserire**
insist **insistere**
inspect **ispezionare**
install **installare**
instruct **istruire**
interrupt **interrompere**
invite **invitare**

J

jump **saltare**

K

keep **tenere**
know (something) **sapere**
know (somebody) **conoscere**

L

laugh **ridere**
learn **imparare**
leave **lasciare, partire**
lie **mentire**
listen **ascoltare**
live **vivere**
look **guardare**
lose **perdere**
lose weight **dimagrire**
love **amare**

M

make **fare**
move **muovere**
must **dovere**

N

notify **avvertire**

O

obey **obbedire**
offer **offrire**
organize **organizzare**

P

paint **dipingere**
pay **pagare**
permit **permettere**
plant **piantare**
play **giocare, suonare**
prefer **preferire**
pretend **pretendere**
prevent **prevenire**
proceed **procedere**
promise **promettere**
propose **proporre**
protect **proteggere**
provide **provvedere**
punish **punire**
put **mettere**

R

rain **piovere**
reach **raggiungere**
read **leggere**
receive **ricevere**
reduce **ridurre**
remain **rimanere**
remember **ricordare**
remove **spostare**
request **richiedere**
resolve **risolvere**
rest **riposare**
result **conseguire**
return **ritornare, tornare**
reunite **riunire**
run **correre**

S

say **dire**
scream **urlare**
see **vedere**

sell **vendere**
send **mandare**
serve **servire**
sew **cucire**
share **condividere**
show **mostrare**
sign **firmare**
sing **cantare**
ski **sciare**
sleep **dormire**
slow down **rallentare**
smile **sorridere**
snow **nevicare**
speak **parlare**
spend **spendere**
start **cominciare**
stay **stare**
stop **fermare**
study **studiare**
substitute **sostituire**
succeed **avere successo**
suffer **soffrire**
swallow **inghiottire**
swim **nuotare**

T

take **prendere**
take off **partire**
taste **assaggiare, gustare**
teach **insegnare**
tell **dire**
think **pensare**
transfer **trasferire**
translate **tradurre**
transmit **trasmettere**
travel **viaggiare**
try **provare**
turn **girare**
turn off **spegnere**

U

understand **capire**
unite **unire**

V

visit   **visitare**
vote   **votare**

W

wait   **aspettare**
walk   **camminare**
wash   **lavare**
wish   **desiderare**
work   **lavorare**
write   **scrivere**